Essentially You @ Work

Essentially You @ Work:
A Career Transition Guide
By Shawn Snelgrove

ISBN 978-0-578-00505-8

Brainstorming à la Mode, Inc. inspires innovative solutions for business challenges with professionals and teams in transition. Bring out your creative best with our career coaching, leadership & team development, facilitation, and consulting services!

PO Box 1337, Boulder, Colorado 80306
www.brainstormingalamode.com
(303) 810-1437
info@brainstormingalamode.com

Table of Contents   **Page Number**

Introduction

Career transition is an opportunity to reconnect to who you are and what really matters. It's a time to take stock and examine your career — what's working, what's not, and why.

If you're looking for your dream job, entering or rejoining the world of work, reeling from a layoff, redefining retirement, planning a new career, or reinvigorating the career you have, zero in on the ways you best contribute to attract work that excites and serves.

Essentially You @ Work: A Career Transition Guide is a framework for career exploration, transition, and self-discovery. It's a workbook designed to help you remember, clarify, and claim who you are, what you love, why you're here, and what's in your way. As Confucius says, "Choose a job you love and you'll never have to work a day in your life."

With over 500 resources, tools, and exercises the following pages provide insight, tips, structure, encouragement, and support to help you make the most of this turning point. Whether you use this workbook as a self-study guide or as a coaching companion tool, you'll explore the internal realms first, and then move with renewed insight and clarity to the external world of applying yourself.

From essence to form, you're inviting the part of you that knows everything to show you the path to greater service and a fulfilling paycheck. With a greater understanding of who you are (and an aligned résumé), you'll gain confidence and be better able to notice and attract opportunities meant for you.

Section 1 helps you receive the wisdom of this moment by considering questions such as:

- How do you appreciate what you're experiencing right now?
- What are your needs and what's the quality of your life?
- Who's supporting you and what constraints are you working with?

Section 2 allows you to remember who you are and what makes you unique by exploring questions such as:

- What are your natural talents? What do you love to do?
- What are your dreams? How do you best serve life?
- What do you value?
- What do you think is possible?

Section 3 enables you to celebrate and face your work history by addressing questions such as:

- What are your career accomplishments to date? What lessons have you learned?
- How do you resolve unfinished business?

Section 4 lets you discover where you can (and want to) be of most service in the marketplace by answering questions such as:

○ What are your marketable skills?
○ How do your personality tendencies align or interfere with the work you seek?
○ What work environment and type suits you? Should you start your own business?
○ What career options are you attracted to?
○ Where and how do you look for a job? Who can help?
○ How does your expertise add value? What are your skills worth?
○ How do you create a great résumé?
○ What can you expect and plan for in interviews?
○ How do you write an effective cover letter?
○ What do you need to change or accept about your professional appearance?

Section 5 helps you to focus your work efforts and be more open to opportunities by responding to questions such as:

○ What are your career goals and next steps? How aligned are you?
○ How do you decide what opportunity is best for you?
○ How do you deal with the resistance inherent in change?
○ How do you keep your spirits up while you're in transition?

You may start at the beginning and work your way through each section, or you may go directly to the subjects that interest you. The degree to which you explore each topic, and in what order, depends on where you want to focus, what you need, how you like to work, and how much time you're willing to invest in your career transition. There are no right or wrong answers, only what's true for you.

Each topic contains:

Inquiry Powerful questions to access your innate wisdom. Sometimes you'll need to sit with a question for a day or two (or longer) to see what arises in your consciousness.

Exercises Activities to engage all your senses and use both hemispheres of your brain, the logical left and the intuitive right. Each starts with a centering technique to enhance the quality and depth of your work.

Completion Box A framework to capture your discoveries and document your learning.

Resources Web sites, books, and other references for digging deeper in areas that interest you or in which you need more information.

Action A place to record one thing you'll commit to doing, being, or thinking as a result of your discoveries.

Quotes Reflections to inspire and remind you of what you already know.

As you explore, you'll consider and apply the mindsets, skill sets, and being sets of conscious career transition in relationship to the timeline of your life. With regards to career, what's internal (who you are) influences what's external (how you show up) in the context of your whole life and the past, present, and future.

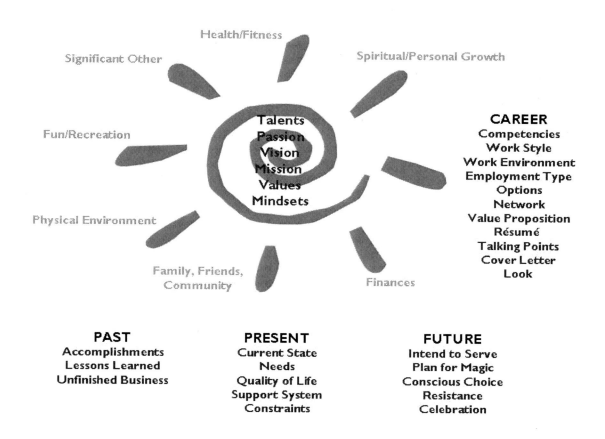

Today's career challenges require creative solutions and conscious choice. Ultimately, you have the answers within you. If you're willing to do your homework, success (as you define it) naturally follows.

Apply what resonates, challenge what doesn't, and let go of the rest!

Transition illuminates if you allow yourself the time, space, and consciousness to experience the light.

Shawn Snelgrove
Founder, Brainstorming à la Mode, Inc.

I. Open the Present

This section helps you access what's available to you right here and right now. It enables you to be more centered in this moment so you can hear your innate wisdom and face your challenges directly. The answers you seek will come to the surface of your consciousness more readily if you are fully present. Instead of starting with the question, "What's next?" ask, "What's now?"

- o Honor Your Current State
- o Know Your Needs
- o Acknowledge the Quality of Your Life
- o Consider Your Support System
- o Accept Your Constraints

"You must be present to win." — unknown

Honor Your Current State

Acknowledge and "be with" wherever you are at this moment in your career. Simply witness what you're feeling, thinking, and sensing inside and experiencing externally, without criticism, judgment, or analysis.

To avoid the counterproductive tendency of focusing on the future or the past (which often generates worry, fear, or guilt), start by simply noticing what's happening. Welcome this time, place, circumstance, and experience as if it were a wise and loving teacher.

Inquiry

1. Check which statement below accurately represents where you are in your career exploration or transition process.

   ☐ Ignoring it ☐ Fighting it ☐ Thinking about it ☐ Just starting
   ☐ Taking a breather ☐ Stuck ☐ Working it ☐ Loving it

2. Circle all the internal (emotions, thoughts, intuitions) and external factors below that are motivating the need for a career change.

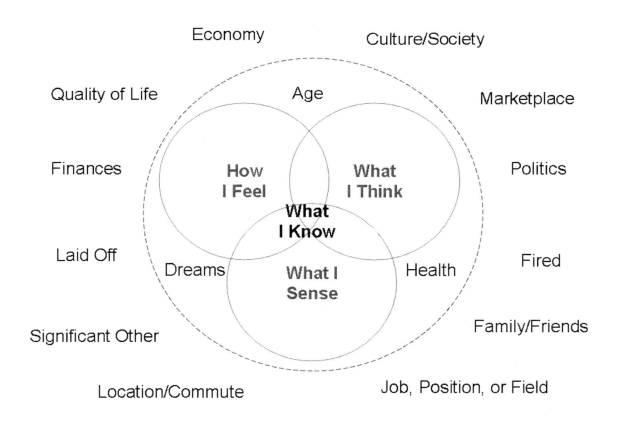

3. Circle the feelings below that most reflect how you <u>really</u> feel about your career, job, business, or work life.

Lost	Immobile	Neutral	Hopeful	Ecstatic
Discouraged	Angry	Centered	Encouraged	Over the top
Apathetic	Frustrated	Aware	Excited	Thrilled

Exercise Normalizing

a. Pause. Take a deep breath. If you can sit outside for a few minutes, do so; if not, find a comfortable place in your home or office. Engage all your senses by observing what each sense is experiencing. If the answer is "nothing" or "I don't know," that's OK. Just acknowledge this and move to the next sense. Check in with your ears (I hear …), eyes (I see …), nose (I smell …), mouth (I taste …), skin (I touch …), and intuition (I perceive …).

b. Any career transition (whether it's planned or not) has predictable phases or "seasons." You may be in a metaphorical winter, when you need time to restore, revitalize, and reconnect to your roots. You may be ready to plant seeds (spring) or enjoy the fruits of your labor (summer). And it may be time to let go (fall). Each season has its gifts! Consider what metaphorical season you're in regarding your career transition and circle it below.

c. Complete the sentence below with as many responses as you can. Just let your thoughts flow with anything that comes to mind.

Of course I'm experiencing what I am in my career because …

My current state of being is …

Resources

Books

- o "Do Nothing" by Steven Harrison
- o "Everything Is Waiting for You" by David Whyte
- o "Mana Keepers" by Kristin Zambucka
- o "Peace Is Every Step" Thich Nhat Hanh
- o "Photography and the Art of Seeing" by Freeman Patterson
- o "Presence" by Peter Senge
- o "Presence Process" by Michael Brown
- o "The Not So Big Life" by Sarah Susanka
- o "The Last Child in the Woods" by Richard Louv
- o "The Power of Full Engagement" by Jim Loehr and Tony Schwartz
- o "The Power of Now" by Eckhart Tolle
- o "The Rhythm of Life" by Matthew Kelly and Patrick Lencioni

Web Sites

- o www.acousticecology.org
- o www.aikiworks.com
- o www.boulderyoga.com
- o www.bksiyengar.com/
- o www.chopra.com
- o www.joanborysenko.com/
- o www.judithlasater.com
- o www.mindtools.com (stress management section)
- o www.nianow.com
- o www.openskyyoga.com
- o www.qi.org/
- o www.spiritualityhealth.com
- o http://stress.about.com/od/stresshealth/a/laughter.htm
- o www.studiobeyoga.com

Other References

- o Classes in mediation, qigong, yoga, tai chi, photography, and nia in your community or at your local fitness center
- o Wellness, stress management, mind-body programs at your local hospital, medical center, lifelong learning or college campus

Action

I commit to doing/being/thinking _____ as a result of my discoveries.

> "A bird doesn't sing because it has an answer.
> It sings because it has a song." — Maya Angelou

Know Your Needs

Needs are fundamental human desires that are requirements, not wants. Identify, understand, acknowledge, and honor your needs before you assess and develop strategies to meet them. For example, a job (a position in exchange for income) meets needs such as financial security and physical well-being. A career (a job with purpose) fulfills additional needs such as meaning, contribution, and growth.

When you articulate your needs clearly and honestly, strategies to meet these needs become more obvious. Then what you manifest or attract will better match what you seek.

Inquiry

1. What needs are paramount for you at this moment? (Circle all that apply on the Needs List below.)

Needs List

Autonomy: choice, financial security, freedom, independence, space, spontaneity

Connection: acceptance, affection, belonging, cooperation, closeness, community, companionship, consistency, consideration, emotional safety, empathy, fairness, inclusion, intimacy, kindness, love, nurturing, reassurance, recognition, respect, security, self-worth, support, trust

Integrity: alignment, honesty

Meaning: awareness, clarity, competence, consciousness, contribution, effectiveness, growth, learning, mourning, purpose, self-expression, serving, wisdom

Peace: beauty, communion, ease, equality, harmony, inspiration, order, spirituality, stability

Play: joy, humor, celebration

Physical Well-Being: air, exercise/movement, food, physical safety, protection, rest, sexual expression, shelter, touch, water

Self-Expression: authenticity, creativity, presence, to be known, understanding

---

2. What do you need physically, emotionally, mentally, spiritually, financially, and socially right now? (Use the Needs List as a guide and fill in the blanks below.)

   ◦ Physical: My body needs …

   ◦ Emotional: The feelings I'm experiencing suggest a need for …

   ◦ Mental: My mind needs …

   ◦ Spiritual: My relationship with my higher self needs …

   ◦ Financial: I need this much money in my bank account to cover my responsibilities …

   ◦ Social: I need this from my family, friends, and community …

Exercise Needs Assessment

a. Center yourself by putting your fingertips from each hand together lightly, lining up thumb to thumb, forefinger to forefinger, etc. Wait until you feel the pulse in all your fingertips. Then consider your career needs.

b. Based on your experiences, think about what you need in your work life at this time. With this consideration in mind, get out some crayons, colored pencils, or colored markers and start doodling in the space below. Express your work needs through a drawing. It doesn't have to be perfect or even good. Simply invite your subconscious mind to speak to you in a picture form. When you're done, reflect on your drawing and what it means to you.

My top five needs for work include …

Resources
Books
- o "First You Have to Row a Little Boat" by Richard Bode
- o "Non-Adversarial Communication: Speaking and Listening From the Heart" by Arlene Brownell and Tom Bache-Wiig
- o "Non-Violent Communication: A Language of Compassion" by Marshall Rosenberg
- o "Theory of Everything" by Ken Wilbur

Web Sites
- o www.braingym.com
- o www.careerplanner.com
- o www.connectionpartners.com
- o www.integralinstitute.com
- o www.iseek.org
- o www.meaingfulcareers.com
- o http://my.jobstreet.com/career/career/tips18.htm
- o www.nvc.org
- o www.maslow.com

Action

I commit to doing/being/thinking _____ as a result of my discoveries.

"Find a need and fill it." — Ruth Stafford Peale

Acknowledge the Quality of Your Life

Your career, business, or job is one part of your whole life. There's a direct correlation between how satisfied you are at work and in the rest of your life. It's important to know where you stand before you define where you're going. As you recognize and accept the quality of your life as it really is, you can build on what's working and make more targeted changes in areas that are not.

Inquiry

1. What do you like about your life right now?

2. What don't you like about your life right now?

Exercise Life Satisfaction Survey

a. Relax a moment by doing some neck rolls. Sit up straight or stand and drop your chin to your chest. Then very slowly move your left ear to your left shoulder. Look up dropping your head back and then lower your right ear to your right shoulder. Repeat with your eyes closed. Then make a few circles in the opposite direction.

b. On a scale of 1–5, rate yourself below by circling the number that best reflects your current level of satisfaction with each aspect of life. When you are done, look at the interrelationship between your career score and the rest of your life.

	1 = Awful		3 = OK		5 = Wonderful
Career	1	2	3	4	5
Health/Fitness	1	2	3	4	5
Finances	1	2	3	4	5
Spiritual/Personal Growth	1	2	3	4	5
Physical Environment	1	2	3	4	5
Family	1	2	3	4	5

	1 = Awful	3 = OK	5 = Wonderful		

Friends/Social	1	2	3	4	5
Community Service/Involvement	1	2	3	4	5
Fun, Recreation, and Play	1	2	3	4	5
Significant Other	1	2	3	4	5

The quality of my life is …

Resources
Books
- o "A Life at Work" by Thomas Moore
- o "Authentic Happiness" by Martin Seligman
- o "It's About Time" by Margaret Wheatly

Web Sites
- o www.aamindell.net/ (Levels of Reality)
- o www.calvert-henderson.com/ (Quality of Life Indicators)
- o www.findyourspot.com/
- o www.gailsheehy.com
- o www.hudsoninstitute.com (Cycle of Renewal)
- o www.internationalliving.com
- o www.oprah.com
- o www.quintcareers.com/work-life_balance_quiz.html
- o www.whatsyouredge.com/products.htm
- o www.worklifebalance.com/

Action

I commit to doing/being/thinking _____ as a result of my discoveries.

"The universe doesn't want you to work hard; it wants you to work well."
— Candace Lienhart

Consider Your Support System

As you grow, evolve, and change, your relationships are affected. Each change you make impacts your family, friends, significant other, children, community, boss, co-workers, staff, clients, etc. Like a pebble that's tossed into a calm lake, your choices create a ripple that influence others and vice versa.

Inquiry

1. Who has expectations or a vested interest in your growth or career path?

2. Who is supportive? Who isn't?

3. With whom do you have spoken or unspoken, formal or informal agreements or contracts to fulfill?

4. What's the universe providing right now in terms of support?

Exercise Object Lessons

a. Sit comfortably and take five deep breaths from your diaphragm while focusing on the air moving in and out of your nostrils. Close your right nostril with the thumb of your right hand and inhale through your left nostril. Then release your thumb while closing the left nostril with the fourth finger of the same hand and exhale out the right. Repeat the cycle for five more breaths.

b. Clear a table or desk so you have some space to work. Consider all the people in your life who are affected by or helping you with your career transition. Include everyone in your orbit such as family members, friends, spiritual teachers, colleagues, bosses, customers, coaches, angels, guides, psychotherapists, teachers, body workers, mentors, neighbors, health care professionals, pets, etc. Make a list.

c. Look around your home and select small objects that represent these people in your life (including yourself). Give yourself some time to consider what object most represents a specific person.

   ◦ For example, you may select a $10 bill for a person who always asks you about money, a paperweight for someone who is a "rock" in your life and always there for you, a crumpled up piece of paper for someone who tends to squash your dreams, or a feather for the angel flying around whispering helpful hints and supporting your growth.

d. Pick up each object/person and consider how you honestly feel about him/her. Does the person make you feel anxious or loved? Is s/he helpful or critical, supportive or concerned? Fill in the boxes below with your discoveries.

Person	Feeling	Discovery

e. Look at all these people in relation to you. Ask yourself, "How do I interact with and rely on my career transition team?" Then arrange the objects in relation to yourself.

f. Look at the 3-D display. What does it reveal about you and your interdependencies? What do you need more of? Less of? From whom?

My support system is …

Resources
Books
- o "Community" by Peter Block
- o "Eat, Pray, Love" by Elizabeth Gilbert
- o "Ishmael" by Daniel Quinn
- o "Life of Pi" by Yan Martel
- o "Listening Is an Act of Love" by Dave Isay
- o "The Relationship Cure" by John M. Gottman

Web Sites
- o www.angelesarrien.com/
- o www.coachfederation.org (Relationship Coaches)
- o www.coachingrelationships.com (Jeannine Lee)
- o http://intuitivesvs.com/
- o www.medicinecards.com
- o www.melodybeattie.com
- o www.myss.com
- o www.soundstrue.com
- o www.therelationshipcoaches.com

Action

I commit to doing/being/thinking _____ as
a result of my discoveries.

"There are friends of time which give our lives continuity and friends of like mind which give our lives possibility." — O Magazine

Accept Your Constraints

You have limitations and realities that will restrict your choices. Some you were born with, some are of your own making, some are imposed, and some are just part of life. Time, debt, physical appearance, family commitments, injury, bills, competing demands, disability, reputation, stereotypes, the economy, and culture are just a few realities that often get in the way of fulfilling career dreams. Instead of ignoring, avoiding, or pretending that constraints don't exist, face them directly. You might be surprised by what your limitations have to offer.

Inquiry

1. What are your current constraints (time, finances, commitments) or the obstacles you need to face at this time regarding your work life?

2. What are the consequences or impact of these constraints on you, your family, and your community?

3. How do your constraints serve you? What do you get from your constraints?

Exercise Career Exploration Time Bank

a. Go to www.youtube.com and type "Life Means So Much" in the search box. Listen to Chris Rice's way of appreciating the time we have. Reflect on the lyrics and bring your insights into the exercise below.

b. Making time for career exploration can be challenging, especially if you're working a full-time job, reeling from a layoff, or supporting a family. To make it a priority, consider the payoff. Use the following table to:

    i.   Write down all the career exploration activities you can do such as brainstorming with a friend, surfing the net and going to networking events.

    ii.   Rate your energy level around each task. For example, when you're updating your resume, is your energy level typically high, medium, or low?

    iii.   Rate how your time investment pays off. For example, when you're researching online, is the payoff (what you and others receive) high, medium, or low?

Time	Career Exploration Activity	Energy Level (high, med, low)	Payoff (high, med, low)

c. When you're done, assess your time account. If writing thank you notes is a high payoff activity, where will you create the space to do the work? If you have too much time on your hands, how will you stay energized? Use the tips below to block time in your schedule for high energy and high payoff career exploration activities.

- Identify the long- and short-term payoffs of career exploration.
- Write down all the reasons it's time for a change.
- Block time on your calendar; make an appointment with yourself.
- Select a high energy time for this work (not 12 a.m. after a long day).
- Work in 60- to 90-minute chunks.
- Color-code your calendar.
- Add an inspirational quote to remind yourself why this time is so important.
- Identify what you have to "say NO to" in order to stick with this commitment.
- Celebrate the hours you invest each day in career exploration.
- Build into your future work the activities that have high energy and payoff.
- Find a buddy to work with and be accountable to.
- Identify everyone and everything that benefits from your career planning time.
- Reclaim parts of your day that are wasted in worry, unfulfilling activity, or stress.
- Identify all the activities that you engage in that make you feel better in the short term but guilty in the long run.
- Add something to do each day that scares you. Take risks in service to your dreams.

The constraints I need to work with include …

Resources

Books

- o "A Room of One's Own" by Virginia Woolf
- o "Crossing the Unknown Sea" by David Whyte
- o "First Things First" by Stephen Covey
- o "Getting Things Done" by Dave Allen
- o "Ordinary Miracles: True Stories About Overcoming Obstacles" by Deborah Labovitz
- o "Leave the Office Earlier" by Laura Strack
- o "Making Work, Work" by Julie Morgenstern
- o "Managing Transitions: Making the Most of Change" by William Bridges
- o "Seven Habits of Highly Effective People" by Stephen Covey
- o "Slow Down to Get More Done" by Marshall J. Cook
- o "Stress for Success" by James E. Loehr

Web Site

- o www.harveymackay.com
- o www.mindtools.com (time management section)
- o www.nationalgeographic.com/xpeditions/lessons/15/g68/obstacles.html
- o www.suzeorman.com (debt)

Action

I commit to doing/being/thinking _____ as a result of my discoveries.

"Most of our obstacles would melt away if, instead of cowering before them, we should make up our minds to walk boldly through them."
— Orison Swett Marden

II. Meet Yourself

This section helps you remember who you are in essence and what motivates you most. As you become more conscious of who you really are, your most rewarding career path can be illuminated from the inside out. Each step you choose to take is then in alignment with the best of you and in service to something greater than you.

o Claim Your Talents
o Remember What You Love
o Have a Dream
o Follow the Call (Even If You Don't Get It)
o Align With Your Values
o Explore Your Mindsets

"Does a flower, full of beauty, light, and loveliness say, 'I'm giving, helping, and serving?' It is! And because it is not trying to do anything, it covers the earth."
— Krishnamurti

Claim Your Talents

The things you do best without thinking describe your innate abilities or gifts. These attributes combine in a way that's unique to you. Talents are ever present because they live in you. They can be developed or denied, applied or hidden, appreciated or disregarded.

Because talents are natural and appear effortless, they are often overlooked or discounted. Organizations and their customers need your talents to thrive. The more you recognize and share your distinctive gifts, the happier you'll be.

Inquiry

1. In what activities do you forget time?

2. What subjects in school and/or tasks at work are effortless and fun?

3. What comes easily to you?

4. What do performance reports or report cards reveal about your strengths?

5. What do clients, friends, bosses, or peers say about your abilities?

6. What are you most knowledgeable about? What information do you love talking about or sharing?

Exercise If You Were …

a. Center yourself by sitting comfortably in a chair. Now stand up without making a sound. If you hear anything, sit down again and observe what made the noise; then try a new method to stand up again without a sound. Keep trying until you achieve this, and notice your energy level, heart rate, and feelings as you do so.

b. Play with a metaphor to see whether you can learn more about yourself and your natural inclinations. For each question, write down what type or brand you'd be and why. Answer with what first comes to mind.

    ○   If you were a car, what kind would you be? Why?

    ○   If you were a game, what would you be? Why?

    ○   If you were a flower, what kind would you be? Why?

    ○   If you were a piece of art, what would you be? Why?

I naturally contribute … (List your talents.)

Resources

Books

- o "What Should I Do With My Life" by Po Bronson
- o "Pathfinders" by Nicholas Lore
- o "Strengths Finder 2.0" by Tom Rath

Web Sites

- o www.anticareer.com
- o www.gregglevoy.com/
- o www.manifestyourpotential.com
- o www.rickjarrow.com
- o www.togetunstuck.com/
- o www.workpassionportal.com

Action

I commit to doing/being/thinking _____ as a result of my discoveries.

> "Be yourself. No one can tell you that you are doing it wrong."
> — James Leo Herlihy

Remember What You Love

Desire is what lights you up. It's an attractor of ideas, people, and revenue. Identify what you're curious about, interested in, and passionate about. Notice what delights you. Consider passions that have stayed with you all your life regardless of job, title, location, or circumstance.

If it's challenging to describe what you love, you may have simply forgotten what brings you joy. You may believe that it's not possible to do what you love for a living, so to explore it seems fruitless. You may have spent so much time focusing on what you don't like that you can't recall what you do like. Or you may discover that your passion has been usurped by cultural, familial, and societal norms, so you've lost what's true for you. If this is the case, it might take some time to reclaim what you love.

Inquiry

1. What are your favorite books, movies, songs, foods, TV shows, magazines, and locations?

2. What people, places, or things energize you?

3. What do you jump out of bed in the morning to do, see, or experience?

4. What don't you like? (Make a dramatic list and then consider opposites.)

Exercise Attraction Scale

a. Focus your attention on your ingoing and outgoing breath. Notice the length of your inhale and exhale. Then see if you can get your inhale to match your exhale. Breathe in for a count of 1, 2, 3, 4 and out for a count of 1, 2, 3, 4. Put your attention on creating a balance between the inhale and exhale. Let your breath lead you to this state of equilibrium.

b. Get conscious about what catches your attention to learn more about what you love. Look around right now in whatever environment you're in and start rating what you see as if you're a magnet.

c. Notice what you are drawn to without having to explain why. Consider things and people as well as colors, shapes, and sizes. Anything in your environment can be scored, such as cars, clothes, images, furniture, scenery, buildings, dogs, trees, equipment, etc. As you assess, notice what you feel. Do you get excited or tired? Do you get a pit in your stomach or expansion in your heart? Does your energy level expand or contract? Are you drawn to the object or repelled by it? Use this scoring system:

1= Repelled   **2** = Neutral   **3** = Attracted

d. Try this activity in different environment for a week and silently rate what you see. Take a walk in your neighborhood, go window shopping, hike in the woods, surf the internet, hang out in a coffee shop saying 1, 2, or 3 in your mind as you notice people, places, and things. Remember: You aren't judging or making a right/wrong or good/bad assessment; you're simply noticing what attracts you and what doesn't.

I love …

Resources
Books
- o "Do What You Love, The Money Will Follow" by Marsha Sinetar
- o "Hitting Your Stride" by Nan S. Russell
- o "It's Only Too Late If You Don't Start Now" by Barbara Sher
- o "The Career Guide for Creative and Unconventional People" by Carol Eikleberry
- o "Work With Passion: How to do what you love for a living" by Nancy Anderson
- o "Whistle While You Work" by Richard Leider

Web Sites
- o www.barbarasher.com/
- o www.odemagazine.com
- o www.selfgrowth.com
- o www.thehappyguy.com

Action

I commit to doing/being/thinking _____ as a result of my discoveries.

"When you want something, all the universe conspires in helping you achieve it." — Paulo Coelho

Have a Dream

Vision is a tangible mental image of a desired future state to attract your desires and provide inspiration through times of challenge.

Life is Good® founders Bert and John Jacobs visualized a contagious grin on T-shirts. The Foundation for a Better Life® envisioned a planet where people were inspired to take responsibility for their actions. Johnny, a downs syndrome grocery bagger, wanted to make a difference. The Wellness Initiative saw yoga in every classroom. David Isay, the founder of StoryCorps® on NPR radio, wanted to honor the stories of life. Sarah, a high-powered executive, imagined a balanced life. Martin Luther King Jr. saw a world "where black men and white men, Jews and gentiles, Protestants and Catholics, joined hands … ." Each had numerous trials and tribulations along the way.

Whether your dream is grand or not, please don't judge its size or scope; just have one. A compelling vision targets your focus, time, and decisions, and it opens your heart and attracts like-minded people to you.

Inquiry

1. What do you yearn for?

2. What's your desired future impact?

3. What do you want the future to look like for yourself, your family, your community, and your world?

4. How will you be in 10 years? Twenty years?

Exercise Vision Board

a. Go to www.americanrhetoric.com/speeches/mlkihaveadream.htm for Martin Luther King Jr.'s speech **or** go to www.youtube.com and type "Paul Potts Canta Opera" in the search field **or** check out http://www.stservicemovie.com/ to learn about Johnny. Listen to Mr. King, Mr. Potts, or Johnny for inspiration to remember your own dream!

b. Collect a stack of your favorite magazines, a large poster board, and a glue stick. Working with the phrase "I have a dream that ...," go through the magazines and cut out pictures and words that fill in the blank. Don't think too much. Just look and cut.

c. Place the words and pictures on your board in whatever design appeals to you. You can add your own drawings or photos if you like.

d. Post this board in an area you'll see frequently. In times of challenge or frustration, look at it and see what happens.

I have a dream that ...

Resources

Books
- o "Creative Visualization" by Shakti Gawain
- o "Finding Your Own North Star" by Martha Beck
- o "The Art of Possibility" by Benjamin Zander
- o "The Dream Manager" by Matthew Kelly

Web Sites
- o www.corporate.disney.go.com
- o www.creativeadvantage.com/visioning.htm
- o www.forbetterlife.org
- o www.lifeisgood.com
- o www.louisehay.com/index.php
- o www.shaktigawain.com/
- o www.storycorps.com
- o www.thedashmovie.com
- o www.thesecret.tv
- o www.wellnessinitiative.com
- o www.wish.org

Action

I commit to doing/being/thinking _____ as a result of my discoveries.

"All our dreams come true if we have the courage to pursue them."
— Walt Disney

Follow the Call (Even If You Don't Get It)

Mission is a touchstone to remind you of the impact you naturally create in the world on a daily basis. It's not what you do, but how you are. It's not something you make up or learn. It's your authentic nature. You contribute simply by being and applying yourself.

A mission is a call to action. It's a quiet voice that constantly reminds you of who you are, why you're here, and how you can be of service to life. It describes essential qualities that you express without effort and follow willingly. Instead of asking the question, "What's my purpose?" or "Why am I here?" try asking, "How can I serve today?" or "What's my next assignment?" or "What needs my attention today?"

Inquiry

1. Where do you feel most needed?

2. What inspires you to action? What's calling you?

3. What keeps coming up in your life? What yearning doesn't go away over the years?

4. What five words best describe the impact you naturally have at work?

Exercise Feedback

a. Read a poem by David Wagoner, David Whyte, or Mary Oliver at www.poets.org. Let the words roll around in your consciousness.

b. From this place of curiosity and wonder, identify three people you enjoyed working with recently. They can be clients, employees, bosses, or peers.

c. Call each person and ask about results you contributed to and what you brought to the job. What do they enjoy about you? Why do they work with you? Write down their specific responses on the next page. "Fun" or "hard worker" isn't enough. You're digging for detailed qualities and examples.

o

o

o

I serve life by ...

Resources

Books

- o "A New Earth: Awakening to Your Life's Purpose" by Eckhart Tolle
- o "Creating the Work You Love" by Rick Jarrow
- o "Man's Search for Meaning" by Viktor Frankl
- o "Quantum Leaps: Seven Workplace Skills for Recreation" by Charlotte Shelton
- o "Stewardship: Choosing Service Over Self-Interest" by Peter Block
- o "The Cultural Creatives: How 50 Million People Are Changing the World" by Paul Ray
- o "The Gift" by Hafiz (translated by Daniel Ladinsky)
- o "The Heart Aroused: Poetry and Preservation of Soul in Corporate America" by David Whyte

Web Sites

- o www.inventuregroup.com (calling cards)
- o www.integrativespirituality.org
- o http://senselist.com/2006/09/06/the-questionnaires-of-james-lipton-bernard-pivot-and-marcel-proust/ (James Lipton's Questionnaire from "Inside the Actor's Studio")
- o www.spiritualcinema.com

Other References

Watch inspiring movies such as "The Lives of Others" or "Simon Birch"

Action

I commit to doing/being/thinking _____ as a result of my discoveries.

"Life is a promise. Fulfill it." — Mother Teresa

Align With Your Values

Values are guiding principles that really matter to you. When you express these intrinsic standards freely, you're more content. When your values are aligned with a profession or organization, you're better able to give your best.

These ideals are often the reason you love what you do, and they often motivate your actions. For example, if you love jogging, you may enjoy the rhythm of your feet on the pavement or the adventure of finding new trails. It may be the feeling of health and fitness, the sensation of wind on your face, or beating the clock that moves you. Whatever you value, you seek to experience.

Inquiry

1. What matters most to you?

2. What can't you live without?

3. What items have you saved, stored, or displayed over the years? What do they mean to you?

4. What were the values of organizations where you enjoyed employment or liked going to work?

Exercise Values Clarification

a. Visit www.youtube.com and type "Magic Beans Peter Mayer" in the search box. Watch, listen, and reflect.

b. Clarify your values by completing the following exercise. Go through each line and identify the degree to which a value matters to you by circling H-High, M-Medium, and L-Low. There is no right or wrong — just what clicks for you.

Values List (© Inside Counts, LLC)

H	M	L	Achievement (attaining goals, sense of accomplishment)
H	M	L	Advancement (progress, promotion)
H	M	L	Adventure (new and challenging experiences, risks)
H	M	L	Appreciation (respect from others, acknowledgement, recognition)
H	M	L	Belonging (involvement, participating with and including others)
H	M	L	Compassion (kindness, concern for others)
H	M	L	Competitiveness (striving to win, being the best)
H	M	L	Creativity (imagination, originality, innovation)
H	M	L	Economic security (steady adequate income)
H	M	L	Enjoyment (fun, pleasure, good times)
H	M	L	Enlightenment (discovery, knowledge, insight, wisdom)
H	M	L	Fame (renown, distinction from others)
H	M	L	Family (close relationships with family members)
H	M	L	Health (physical and mental well-being; fitness)
H	M	L	Independence (freedom and autonomy)
H	M	L	Inner peace (being in harmony with self and others; tranquility)
H	M	L	Integrity (honesty, doing the right thing, behaviors align with beliefs)
H	M	L	Loyalty (commitment, dedication, steadfastness to cause or entity)
H	M	L	Justice (equality, civil rights, human freedom)
H	M	L	Personal growth (learning, realizing potential, self-discovery)
H	M	L	Power (influence, importance, authority)
H	M	L	Relationships (community, friends, connection with others)
H	M	L	Reliability (responsibility, dependability)
H	M	L	Self-esteem (belief in your abilities, self-respect, trusting self)
H	M	L	Service (helping others, making a difference, bettering society)
H	M	L	Spirituality (faith, religious beliefs, regular spiritual practice)
H	M	L	Structure (being organized; having systems, order, boundaries)
H	M	L	Teamwork (collaboration, cooperation, creating unity)
H	M	L	Trust (being trustworthy, creating trusting relationships, acting consistently according to values)
H	M	L	Vitality (sense of aliveness, energy, positive can-do attitude)
H	M	L	Wealth (affluence, getting rich, having what you want, abundance)

c. Circle your top five personal values by looking at the values you rated with a High. To check that your values are "actual" and not just desired, preferred, or imposed, answer these questions:

  o For your top five, find an example in your day planner that reflects each value.

  o If someone who didn't know you looked at the way in which you spent your time, what would s/he say are your actual values?

I treasure … (List top five values.)

Resources

Books

- ○ "Appreciative Inquiry" by David L. Cooperrider
- ○ "Leadership and Self-Deception" by The Arbinger Institute
- ○ "Success With Soul" by Doris Pozzi
- ○ "Think on These Things" by Jiddu Krishnamurti

Web Sites

- ○ http://career-advice.monster.com/selfassessment/Work-Values-Checklist/home.aspx
- ○ www.career-test.biz/
- ○ www.compass4you.com (Susan Hadinger)
- ○ www.insidecounts.com (Amy Felix-Reese)
- ○ www.quintcareers.com/workplace_values.html
- ○ www.risingtides-coach.com (Deirdre Dalton-Brodeur)
- ○ www.stephencovey.com

Action

I commit to doing/being/thinking _____ as a result of my discoveries.

> "We can tell our real values by looking at our checkbook stubs."
> — Gloria Steinem

Explore Your Mindsets

Mindsets are your mental maps — the way in which you navigate the world. They're a group of beliefs, opinions, ideas, programs, cultural expectations, and experiences that consciously and unconsciously shape your life. Because many of your mindsets are formed before you're eight years old, some of this "auto-pilot" thinking may be outdated, illogical, and even inaccurate.

Engage your creative mind by becoming more aware of how you think. Your thoughts are powerful. They attract circumstances into your life and influence what you feel and how you act. To expand your career possibilities, you may need to change your mind.

Inquiry

1. What are your mindsets about work itself? (Circle all the statements that apply and/or add your own.)

   ○ I work to make money — that's all.
   ○ Work is work and I'd rather be playing.
   ○ I deserve to have a job. I'm entitled. It's a human right.
   ○ It's how I contribute and serve life. It's how I apply myself.
   ○ It's my identity. It's who I am.
   ○ The word *work* doesn't fit for me. I love what I do for a living.
   ○ It's a necessary evil.
   ○ My career is my life's work.
   ○ I deserve to have fulfilling work.
   ○ My job affords me the life I want.
   ○
   ○
   ○

2. What's your career heritage? How do the mindsets you learned from your family, culture, and the society that you were born into serve you today? How do they not?

Exercise Playing With Perspectives

a. Stand up with both feet solidly on the ground. Move your hips from right to left keeping your feet in place. When you have a rhythm going swing your arms in the same direction as your hips twisting at your waist a bit. Then add your head looking over your shoulder in the same direction as your hips and arms. Let your eyes follow the movement right to left. Release any tension by swinging for a minute or so.

b. Consider your mindsets or beliefs about finding work in today's economy and marketplace. As you read each statement below, try it on like a coat or pair of shoes. Notice what happens to your body posture, breath, emotions, and physique as you explore different ways of thinking about what's possible. Try on all the perspectives, and then check the one that most represents your current career exploration mindset.

   ○ I don't have the experience or education to do what I love.
   ○ I'm too old/young to have a career.
   ○ There isn't any work out there, especially in this economy.
   ○ Everyone wants to be a _____.
   ○ The perfect position is waiting for me.
   ○ Opportunities abound.
   ○ My expertise adds value so I'm needed somewhere.
   ○ It's been years since I've had to look for work.
   ○ Other (Make up another perspective)

c. How does this mindset serve you? What do you get from thinking in this way?

d. Consider another perspective you'd like to experiment with this week. Ask yourself, "What is possible if I wear this other coat or walk in these different shoes?" Try on the different viewpoints again, and select one from the list below that you're willing to experiment with.

   ○ My experience and expertise is needed in _____.
   ○ There **is** something out there for me.
   ○ Opportunities abound.
   ○ I can best serve life in _____ field.
   ○ It's effortless.
   ○ If it's mine, it's mine. If not, something even better is coming.
   ○ The perfect position is waiting for me.
   ○ Other (Make up another perspective.)

I'll experiment with the following perspective this week…

Resources
Books
- o "Change Your Thoughts, Change your Life" by Wayne W. Dyer
- o "Co-Active Coaching" by Laura Whitworth and Phil Sandahl
- o "Culture Code" by Clotaire Rapaille
- o "Illusions" by Richard Bach
- o "Mutant Message" by Marlo Morgan
- o "Overcoming Job Burnout" by Dr. Beverly Potter
- o "Paradigms: The Business of Discovering the Future" by Joel Barker
- o "Play to Win" by Larry and Hersh Wilson
- o "Power vs. Force: The Hidden Determinants of Human Behavior" by David Hawkins
- o "Reclaiming the Fire" by Dr. Steven Berglas
- o "The Power of Story" by Jim Loehr
- o "The Work of Katie Byron" by Katie Byron
- o "Think and Grow Rich" by Napolean Hill
- o "Way of the Peaceful Warrior" by Dan Millman
- o "Zen and the Art of Making a Living" by Laurence Boldt

Web Sites
- o www.agewave.com
- o www.blindspottest.com
- o www.danielgoleman.info
- o www.davidicke.com
- o www.ishmael.org
- o www.kahunakindergarden.com
- o www.seussville.com
- o www.ted.com
- o www.whatthebleep.com
- o www.zeitgeistmoive.com

Action

I commit to doing/being/thinking _____ as a result of my discoveries.

> "Energy follows thought; we move toward, but not beyond, what we can imagine." — Dan Millman

III. Clean Up Your Work History

This section focuses on organizing, recognizing, and celebrating what you've achieved and learned in your career so far while completing what's still unresolved. This way, you can move forward more enthusiastically and consciously without bringing emotional baggage, regret, or worry with you.

- o Acknowledge Accomplishments
- o Identify Lessons Learned
- o Resolve Unfinished Business

"Strive to learn, before you die, from what you run, and to, and why." — unknown

Acknowledge Accomplishments

Identify and recognize your contributions. Take stock of the impact you've had so far at work, at home, and in the community. Give yourself credit for what you've achieved despite constraints, challenges, or upbringing.

Inquiry

1. What are your major accomplishments in your life so far?

2. What are some specific career highlights?

3. What are some specific examples where you overcame an obstacle to get or create what you wanted or the world needed?

4. How has your presence (just being who you are) made a difference to someone, someplace, or something?

5. What coincidences, synchronicities, or surprises did you capitalize on?

Exercise Recognizing Yourself

a. Before you begin this exercise, go to an art museum or gallery, or visit some online artist or photographer Web sites, such as the ones below. Focus on beauty, creativity, self-expression, and thinking outside the box; then consider your own accomplishments.

www.estaz.net	www.kutzkies.bigstep.com	www.sundancephoto.com
www.maggietaylor.com	http://users.skynet.be/J.Beever/	www.storypeople.com
www.nesegallery.com	www.xmarkjenkinsx.com/nature.html	www.sticks.com

b. Deepen your acknowledgement of your contributions in the world of work by doing a few of the following activities:
   o Go through your files and make a list of all your "wins."
   o Meet a colleague, sibling, or friend to brainstorm about your contributions.
   o Go to the Web sites of companies you've worked for and write down all the specific ways you contributed to their growth.
   o Go through old photo albums and list what you feel good about.
   o Look at your résumé and write some specific results you achieved at each job.
   o Draw a certificate of accomplishment for yourself.
   o Find a song that best represents your contributions and dance to it.
   o Write down everything you did that made you happy last year.
   o Google yourself.
   o Read old yearbooks and report cards and see what teachers and friends wrote.
   o Look around your home or office and note your contributions.
   o Write a poem for yourself or create a recognition ritual of your own.
   o Walk in the woods and find an object such as a pinecone, a rock, or a leaf that reminds you of your contributions.
   o Watch the movie "It's a Wonderful Life" and track your own impact in the world.

I'm proud of my accomplishments because …

Resources

Books
   o "Rivers and Tides" by Andy Goldsworthy
   o "Simple Abundance" by Sarah Ban Breathnach
   o "The Power of Positive Thinking" by Norman Vincent Peale
   o "Wisdom: 365 Thoughts From Indian Masters" by Danielle Follmi

Web Sites
   o www.bucketbook.com
   o www.charthouse.com
   o www.complimentday.com

Action

I commit to doing/being/thinking _____ as a result of my discoveries.

"I can live for months on a good compliment." — Mark Twain

Identify Lessons Learned

Get more conscious about experiences of your life that are unconscious, pushed away, or hidden in your being. Instead of running from, avoiding, ignoring, or beating yourself up for the difficult times, people, or situations of your past, face them all.

JK Rowling was divorced, homeless, and jobless before writing the Harry Potter series. Henry Ford, the founder of Ford Motor Company, went bankrupt five times. Dr. Seuss was rejected 20 times when he tried to publish "Green Eggs and Ham." NBA basketball star Michael Jordan was rejected from his high school team for not being good enough. Elvis Presley got an F in music.

Consider what you learned from your lessons and forgive yourself.

Inquiry

1. List all the career or work experiences you don't talk about.

2. What do these experiences have in common? Is there a pattern to the events or way of thinking?

3. Think of someone you admire and identify three challenges s/he overcame.

Exercise Work History Review

a. Stand for a moment before you begin this activity. Focus on your skeletal system and see whether you can stand still and upright using only 10% muscle. See what muscles you can relax and how it feels to balance on your bones.

b. Look over your résumé or think about your work history. Go through the list of jobs and underline the positions that make you nervous or that you hope an interviewer won't ask you about. For each underlined job, ask yourself, "What is it about this work experience that makes me anxious?" Look for experiences such as these:

   o A difficult boss
   o An emotional departure
   o A change in leadership
   o An unethical act
   o Poor performance

- Lack of recognition
- Misaligned values (yours with the company or personnel)
- Assignments over your head
- A lie or a boundary issue (in a relationship or role)
- Justifications
- Mistreatment
- Anything you label "a failure," whether or not it's true
- "Mistakes"
- Arguments, burned bridges or misunderstandings

c. List your insights below, along with what you learned from these experiences.

Insight	Learning

The following lessons are helpful today because …

Resources

Books
- "The Alchemist" by Paulo Coelho
- "The Flowering of Human Consciousness" by Eckhart Tolle
- "Illuminati" by Marianne Williamson

Web Sites
- www.beliefnet.com
- www.selfgrowth.com

Action

I commit to doing/being/thinking _____ as a result of my discoveries.

"Where you stumble, there your treasure lies." — Joseph Campbell

Resolve Unfinished Business

Release unresolved experiences, stories, indiscretions, "mistakes," wrongdoings, and "failures" from your past. Everything is up for review — even expectations such as the lists in your head of everything you thought you'd do with your life.

Use the energy of shame, frustration, blame, conflict, guilt, and anger to make amends and create space for something new. It takes a lot of energy to hide transgressions, ignore regret, or carry unfulfilled dreams. Resolution is a worthwhile choice.

Inquiry

1. What story, experience, or person do you need to release, let go of, or change?

2. With whom do you have unfinished business?

3. What are all the ways you've "failed" yourself or others?

4. What opportunities did you "miss" and/or what careers did you not pursue? Why?

Exercise Close the Loop

a. Go to www.quotegarden.com and look at quotes on forgiveness. Find one that resonates and ponder it for a few minutes.

b. Make a list of all the people, teams, customers, or organizations that you have issues with, including yourself. It may be someone you disappointed, an action you regret, an outcome you contributed to but never "owned" or poor judgment. Look for times you tried to unsuccessfully force an outcome, resisted change, or limited your self-expression.

c. Try one of the following ideas to claim and resolve the difficulty:

- Speak your truth to the person in your imagination as if s/he is sitting in the same room with you.
- Write an honest, heartfelt letter to the person, and then send it or burn it.
- Imagine you could go back in time and do something different. What would it be? Pretend you can fix it and rewrite the past by enacting it as you would have liked it to be in your mind.
- Make a psychic phone call or call for an investigation (see www.kahunakindergarden.com in the Sharing the Good Stuff section).
- Hire an ethical healer or counselor to help you process the incident or better understand the relationship.
- Call the person and apologize directly, keeping attention on him/her not yourself.
- Create a forgiveness ceremony or ritual of your own design.
- Identify your own "shame and blame" behaviors and choose more accountable ways to respond so there is less to forgive in the future.
- Consider how you contributed to the situation or relationship and forgive yourself for your own ignorant behavior.
- List everything you promised yourself and decide what's current and what you can cross off.
- Identify emotional expectations and attachments and let them go.
- Write a heartfelt thank you note.
- Try the mantra from "Zero Limits": "I love you, I'm sorry, forgive me, thank you."
- Use the apology from "The Last Lecture": "I'm sorry. I was wrong. How do I make it right?"
- Experiment with ideas from "Energetic Boundaries": Explore the ways you were a surrogate or conduit for someone else's emotions, experience, or homework and return what you've taken on that doesn't belong to you.
- Explore different indigenous and religious traditions of forgiveness ceremonies and use one that resonates for you.
- Learn and apply the ancient Hawaiian Ho'Oponopono method "to make right."
- Ask yourself in a loving manner, "How did I contribute to this conflict?"

I forgive myself for …

Resources
Books
- o "Energetic Boundaries" by Karla McLaren (CD from www.soundstrue.com)
- o "Illuminata: A Return to Prayer" by Marianne Williamson
- o "The Last Lecture" by Randy Pausch
- o "Play To Win" by Larry Wilson (Stop-Challenge-Choose)
- o "Spirits of the Earth: A Guide to Native American Nature Symbols, Stories, and Ceremonies" by Robert Lake-Thom
- o "The Art of Forgiveness, Loving Kindness, and Peace" by Jack Kornfield
- o "The Power of Story" by Jim Loehr
- o "The Return of Merlin" by Deepak Chopra
- o "Zero Limits" by Joe Vitale

Web Sites
- o www.aa.org
- o www.adyashanti.org
- o www.gangaji.com
- o http://www.ancienthuna.com/ho-oponopono.htm
- o www.intutivesvs.com (Kathy Reider)
- o www.kahunakindergarden.com (Candace Lienhart)
- o www.lyngregory.com
- o http://www.mayoclinic.com/health/forgiveness/MH00131
- o www.marriane.com
- o www.medicine-eagle.com
- o www.soundstrue.com
- o http://www.spiritualityhealth.com/newsh/items/selftest/item_232.html
- o www.twoblueherons.net (Mariah Martin)
- o www.wavemakercoaching.com
- o www.zerolimits.com

Other References
Counselors, psychotherapists, coaches, body workers and healers that have been recommended by friends or colleagues and with whom you resonate.

Action

I commit to doing/being/thinking _____ as a result of my discoveries.

> "Until you make peace with who you are,
> you'll never be content with what you have." — Doris Mortman

IV. Fill a Marketplace Need

This section helps you clarify what you offer, where the marketplace needs you, and how your talents add value. It's where you translate your inner realizations into a language and format the marketplace can understand, consider, and purchase. It's also how you make sure that who you are on the inside and who you are on the outside is congruent.

- o Share Your Core Competencies
- o Match Your Style
- o Identify Your Optimal Work Environment
- o Choose Your Employment Type
- o Explore Your Options
- o Tap Your Network
- o Create a Value Proposition
- o Refine Your Résumé
- o Develop Talking Points
- o Target Cover Letters
- o Update Your Looks

"Life is an exciting business, and most exciting when it is lived for others." — Helen Keller

Share Your Core Competencies

Competencies are the specific ways you contribute and add value in the marketplace. They describe the observable knowledge, skills, talents, and abilities you've developed and applied.

Competence is different from confidence. Competence is a fact without arrogance. It's what you excel in or what you're really good at doing, saying, intuiting, or thinking that has value (people will pay for it) and meets an organizational functional need. If you downplay your abilities for fear of being arrogant or overzealously promote your competencies for fear of being inadequate, learn to acknowledge the facts. Know what you do well; then identify how others benefit specifically from your expertise.

Inquiry

1. What's the central theme or focus of your work experience and expertise so far?

2. What capabilities does your résumé highlight?

3. What everyday tasks are you really good at? (List everything, even things such as grocery shopping, changing oil, or doing your taxes.)

Exercise Identifying competencies

a. Walk through your neighborhood and see whether anyone is out working in the yard or shoveling snow, or see what your children, spouse, or friends are up to. Ask whether you can help them out for 30 minutes or so. Notice what skills you apply as you do so.

b. To identify your marketable competencies, use any or all of the following approaches:

Talents and gifts inventory	Use your discoveries on page 28-30 to convert your innate talents and gifts to marketable skills. Change the language or use verbiage that aligns with the field work you seek.
Professional career skills inventory	Determine the required skills for the profession or career that you are in or pursuing. Research online and list all the skills required of your profession. Then rate your competency level high, medium, or low for each item.
Knowledge-based skills inventory	Identify your basic, interpersonal, judgment, management, numerical, reasoning, technical, and computer skills learned through past experience and education and see what careers match your competencies. Go to http://www.iseek.org/sv/Skills?outId=12403 or another skills-assessment Web site and rate yourself in basic, communication, hearing/vision, interpersonal, judgment, management, movement, numerical, reasoning, problem-solving, and technical skills.
Transferable skills	Assess the skills you have from life activities — such as classes, projects, parenting, hobbies, and sports — that you bring with you to any job. Think in terms of people skills, data skills, and working-with-things skills. If this is challenging, go to a career site such as www.monster.com or http://www.amby.com/worksite/cjs/cjsbook2/skill6d.htm and look at skills lists, job descriptions, or resources to get ideas.
Functional skills	Consider skills that contribute to specific functions in any organization, such as strategic planning, research and development, operations, customer service, purchasing, PR, marketing, sales, finance, human resources, legal, information technology, and administrative.

c. Select your top five core competences (what you're really great at) and write them below. Instead of considering all your strengths, isolate the competencies that energize you and make you feel most alive. Look for the central themes of your expertise and what you enjoy contributing, not everything you can do well.

Competency	Example
1.	
2.	
3.	
4.	
5.	

d. For each of your top five competencies, write down one or two specific examples of how using that skill made a difference, felt good, or generated a valuable outcome for a person, team, or organization. Using the following examples as a guide, add one example to each competency above.

Conflict management: Helped mitigate a potential deal breaker with my sales team and new client to secure a $100,000 sale and build relationship.

Creativity: Generated five innovative strategies for new product launch with R&D team before deadline and within budget.

Programming: Converted a five-day, manual, paper-intensive registration process to one-day automated, online service that saved the company $500,000 and improved customer satisfaction scores by 53%.

My top five core competencies are …

Resources
Books
- o "Career Guide for Creative and Unconventional People" by Carol Eikleberry
- o "Passages" by Gail Sheehy
- o "What Color Is Your Parachute" by Richard Nelson Bolles

Web Sites
- o http://amby.com/worksite/cjs/cjsbook2/skill6d.htm
- o www.careerjournal.com
- o www.gregglevoy.com/
- o www.iseek.com
- o http://online.onetcenter.org/find/
- o http://owl.english.purdue.edu/owl/resource/626/01/
- o www.quintcareers.com/transferable_skills_set.html
- o www.jobstar.org
- o www.rileyguide.com

Action

I commit to doing/being/thinking _____ as a result of my discoveries.

"We are all too much inclined to walk through life with our eyes shut. There are things all around us, and right at our very feet, that we have never seen, because we have never really looked." — Alexander Graham Bell

Match Your Style

Style is the manner in which you apply yourself, especially in times of stress. It isn't who you are or your nature; it's the way in which you've learned to show up. When you understand your temperament, behavioral patterns or personality tendencies, it's easier to attract work that matches your disposition.

This self-awareness also enables you to identify what you need to learn or change to get more of what you want and give more of what others need. If your style overrides your authenticity, this awareness will illuminate your growth opportunities.

Inquiry

1. On a good day at work, how do you talk, act, and listen?

2. On a bad day at work, what behavior or way of thinking shows up that you wish wouldn't?

3. What personality traits of yours are <u>and</u> are not aligned with your career arena or occupation?

Exercise Assessment Tools

a. Slow down for a moment. Get a raisin or piece of dried fruit. Sit and take one full minute to eat the raisin/dried fruit. As you do so, close your eyes. Fully taste its sweetness and experience its nourishment. Focus on chewing slowly. Notice what comes into your consciousness as you do so.

b. Select one of the assessment tools below and use the input to learn more about yourself, your tendencies, and what careers match your profile. If you already have assessment results, re-examine them.

   o **Keirsey Temperament Sorter II (KTS-II)** Identify your disposition to be an artisan, guardian, rational, or idealist at <u>www.advisorteam.com</u>. The online test is $14.95. Bundle with Campbell Interest and Skill Survey for $29.95.

   o **Campbell Interest and Skill Survey (C)** Learn which careers best match your aptitudes with <u>www.advisorteam.com</u>. The online test is $19.95. Bundle with KTS-II for $29.95.

- o **Myers-Briggs Career Test** Discover your personality type and what professions suit your type at www.discoveryourpersonality.com. This online test is $60-$65.

- o **Astrological Birth Chart** Use your sun, rising, and moon signs as learning tools and guides. For charting and interpretation, explore Susan Miller's Web site at www.mypersonalhoroscope.com. The cost is $44.95.

- o **StrengthsFinder** Find your top five themes of talent by taking the Gallup assessment. Purchase the book "StrengthsFinder 2.0 at www.strengthfinder.com for $9.95.

- o **People Styles at Work** Find out whether you're amiable, driver, expressive, or analytical and how to work better with all styles. Go to www.amazon.com to purchase the book, which contains the self-assessment. The cost is $13.57.

- o **John Holland Personality Types** Realistic, investigative, artistic, social, enterprising, and/or conventional? Get the Self-Directed Search® Interpretive report to learn about yourself and your educational and life/career choices by going to www.self-directed-search.com. The cost is $9.95.

- o **The Riso-Hudson Enneagram Type Indicator (RHETI)** Find out whether your personality type or nature is a reformer, helper, achiever, individualist, investigator, loyalist, enthusiast, or challenger. Go to www.enneagraminstitute.com to take the RHETI test. From the menu on the home page, click Free RHETI sampler, or take the Full RHETI enneagram test for $10.

c. After you receive or re-examine a report, write down your discoveries and thoughts here:

> **My style enables me to …**

Resources
Books
- "Birth Order Book" by Dr. Kevin Leman
- "Emotional Genius: Discovering the Deepest Language of the Soul" by Karal McLaren
- "The Essential Enneagram" by David Daniels, M.D., and Virginia Price, Ph.D.
- "From Fixation to Freedom" by Eli Jaxon Bear
- "Star Signs at Work" by Debbie Burns
- "The Secret Language of Birthdays" by Gary Goldschneider and Joost Eiffers

Web Sites
- www.careerkey.org
- www.careermaze.com
- www.careerpath.com
- www.careerplanner.com
- www.enneasight.com (Renee Rosario)
- www.improvenow.com
- www.knowyourtype.com
- www.livecareer.com
- http://personal.ansir.com/test.htm
- www.queendom.com
- http://similarminds.com/
- www.testingroom.com
- www.thecareerkey.com
- http://www.truecolorscareer.com/quiz.asp

Action

I commit to doing/being/thinking _____ as
a result of my discoveries.

> "The constitution only gives people the right to pursue happiness.
> You have to catch it yourself." — Ben Franklin

Identify Your Optimal Work Environment

Work environment is the location, type of workplace, people who surround you, and way in which you work that best suits you and enables you to perform optimally. It's important to be honest with yourself so you can explore and attract not only the work you desire but also the quality of life you deserve. And if you choose to take a position that isn't in the "perfect" environment, you can make conscious adjustments.

Inquiry

1. In what location and how many miles from home would you like to work?

2. In what type of work setting? (Check all that apply and add your own.)

❑Corporate office	❑Field	❑Retail	❑Agriculture
❑Plant/Factory	❑Home office	❑Theatre	❑Library
❑Medical	❑Educational	❑Studio	❑Construction
❑R&D	❑Outdoors	❑Religious	❑Indoors
❑Gym	❑ In a Vehicle	❑	❑
❑	❑	❑	❑

3. In a given day, what percentage of the time are you willing to be: (Add percentages to equal to 100% for each row.)

On computer/phone	_____	vs.	Off the computer/phone	_____
In the office	_____	vs.	Out of the office	_____
With people	_____	vs.	Solo	_____
In town	_____	vs.	On the road	_____

4. In what type of work energy are you most productive **and** engaged? (Check all that apply and add your own.)

❑High, fast paced	❑Calm, soothing	❑Frenetic, always changing
❑Stable	❑Fun, creative, colorful	❑Simple, clean, modern
❑Productive	❑Diverse	❑

5. Who are "your people"? What types of co-workers, bosses, employees, and clients do you want to work with? What qualities do they have?

Exercise Ideal Day Visualization

a. Relax by tensing or squeezing your entire body, including making fists with both hands and scrunching up your face. Hold your breath for five seconds, and then release and relax your breath and all your muscles. Repeat three times.

b. Find a quiet, private location. Close your eyes and picture your ideal workday. What does the work environment look like? Who's around? How do you move through the day? What type of work are you doing? What type of equipment are you using? What are you talking about? With whom are you working? Whom are you serving? What's the pace? What is the result of your efforts? How much money are you making? What does your face look like? Give yourself at least five minutes to envision this. Pretend you're actually in the environment. If you get stuck, remember a time at work when you felt content and fulfilled. Describe the job, the people, and the environment at that time.

I work best in the following environment …

Resources

Books
- o "Happy Hour Is 9-5" by Alexander Kjerulf
- o "Lighting the Eye of the Dragon" by Dr. Baolin Wu
- o "Office Feng Shui: Creating Harmony in Your Work Space" by Darrin Zeer

Web Sites
- o www.greatday.com
- o http://money.cnn.com/magazines/fortune/bestcompanies/2007/
- o www.osha.gov/SLTC/etools/computerworkstations/wkstation_enviro.html
- o http://positivesharing.com/2006/10/10-seeeeeriously-cool-workplaces
- o www.thecoolhunter.net/design/CREATIVE-WORK-ENVIRONMENTS---Do-you-work-in-one-/

Action

I commit to doing/being/thinking _____ as a result of my discoveries.

"Rediscovering the beauty of existence, and of our planet, and of our own species — this is where we get our energy back." — Matthew Fox

Choose Your Employment Type

If you're wondering whether self-employment is for you, it's a good time to consider the realities of small business. Long hours, cash flow challenges, irregular income, and high risk are inherent in small business. Greater influence over the quality of your life, as well as more independence and freedom, are also possible. Many small businesses fail, not because people don't have good ideas, products, or services, but because they aren't conscious of what and how long it takes to succeed.

Some people have an aptitude for running their own business, and others learn what it takes because a mission or need motivates them. Increase your odds of success by understanding the realities and illusions of self-employment. Face what it really takes to be an entrepreneur instead of spending your energy in fantasy or delusion.

Inquiry

1. What is it about starting a business, doing your own thing, or being your own boss that's appealing right now?

2. What do you gain by pursing this dream? What do you lose by not pursuing it?

3. What would your workday be like if you acted as if you were self-employed (regardless of whether you are or not)?

Exercise Is Self-Employment for Me?

a. Go online and read stories of successful business people on Web sites such as the ones listed below. As you read the stories, consider whether you're willing to go through the process of starting and running a small business yourself.

   http://www.businessweek.com/smallbiz/successstories/like
   http://www.score.org/success_stories.html
   http://www.entrepreneur.com/startingabusiness/successstories/index.html

b. Take the self-assessment below. Place an X under the heading that best reflects your experience for each statement. Rate yourself as you actually are, not as you'd like to be. If someone watched you in your life or on the job, what would s/he observe?

	Not Me	Me	Definitely Me
I loved earning money as a child.			
I thrive on challenge, adventure, and risk.			
I'm **not** dependent on a steady paycheck.			
I'm generally confident and competent.			
I'm a self-starter, go-getter, and independent thinker.			
I grew up around entrepreneurs and small business owners.			
I've always loved to work.			
I think outside or ignore "the box."			
I don't spend money unless I have it.			
I enjoy talking with others about my work.			
I'm happiest when pursuing my dreams.			
I thrive on chaos and don't need much sleep.			
I'm organized and creating work systems is natural.			
My idea or talent makes the world a better place.			
I've made money in the past with this idea or talent.			
I have a market or niche in mind.			
I know the need(s) my offering fills in the marketplace.			
My marketplace is abundant — there's plenty for all.			
People ask for my help in this niche all the time.			
I use business skills every day.			
I trust the universe to support my efforts.			
I have two years of savings to live on.			

c. The more x's you have in the Me and Definitely Me columns, the more you have what it takes to start a business. If, despite your scores, all this sounds exciting and motivating and you can't wait to get started, go for it. Create a business plan today (see below for a template). If most of your x's are in the Not Me column, you'll need lots of perseverance, support, and training, as well as a detailed business plan and a very compelling idea or mission, to pull off starting your own business.

d. If starting a business is right for you at this time, begin putting your ideas on paper into a business plan framework. Use the following template as a guide, or explore online resources listed in the Resources section. Then hire a business coach!

Business Plan Template

<u>Company Description</u> Describe the vision, mission, values, services, goals, customers, and core competencies of your company.

<u>Market Analysis</u> Describe the marketplace and customer needs.

<u>Competitive Assessment</u> Describe the relevant offerings and price point of your top three competitors.

<u>Products and Services</u> Describe the features, benefits, and advantages of your unique product, service, or talent.

<u>Sales and Marketing</u> Describe your brand, value proposition, and marketing strategy.

<u>Operations</u> Describe the key functions of your business and how you'll run it.

<u>Management and Organization</u> Describe who will manage and organize the main functions of your business. Include expertise and support systems needed.

<u>Financial Requirements</u> Describe start-up costs, operational costs, and estimated profit margins.

<u>Business Structure</u> Describe whether you're going to be a sole proprietor, LLC, Sub-S, or C-Corp and why.

At this point, I'm choosing _____ (type of employment) because …

Resources

Books

- "8 Patterns of Highly Effective Entrepreneurs" by Brent Bowers
- "E-Myth Revisited" by Michael Gerber
- "The Diamond Cutter: The Buddha on Managing Your Business and Your Life" by Geshe Michael Roach

Web Sites

- www.allbusiness.com/
- www.entrepreneur.com/interstitial/default.html
- www.fasttrac.org
- www.getclientsnow.com
- www.hidden-wealth-keys.com/business-structure.html
- www.inc.com
- www.quickmba.com/law/org/
- www.sba.gov
- www.score.org
- www.smartbiz.com/
- www.valuebasedmanagement.net
- www.workhappy.net

Business Coaches

- www.coachfederation.org
- www.insidecounts.com
- www.risingtides-coach.com
- www.whatsyouredge.com

Action

I commit to doing/being/thinking _____ as a result of my discoveries.

"If you woke up breathing, congratulations! You have another chance."
— Andrea Boydston

Explore Your Options

Research, research, research. Notice, notice, notice. Exploring your options is like a treasure hunt. Each clue reveals the next. Start looking for, talking to, and investigating all the possibilities of where your competencies are needed.

As you explore (on the computer and out in the world), you'll receive new ideas, meet new contacts, and expand your options. You'll also better understand the requirements of what you seek and your constraints. The prize for your efforts may be an insight, a contact, a lesson, an answer, a magical hour, or a pot of gold that belongs to only you. As opportunities arise during this process, follow them.

Inquiry

1. If you had all the time and money in the world, what would you do?

2. What industries, organizations, products, and services interest you?

3. What arena do you want to play in?

   o Employed by someone else or self-employed?
   o For-profit or not-for-profit?
   o Volunteer or employed?
   o Small biz or big biz?
   o Government or private sector?
   o National or international?

4. What occupations or professions interest you?

5. What departments (operations, strategy, finance, customer service, human resources, information technology, admin, legal, etc.) and roles/job titles are you considering?

6. What training or education would you love to pursue at this time?

7. In what industry can you be of the most service?

8. What career or type of work do you **not** want to pursue?

9. What are your nighttime dreams revealing about your career options?

10. Whom do you "really" work for and why do you work?

Exercise Research, Get Out, Research, Get Out, Research

a. Get in a "service" frame of mind. Fill up with an attitude of gratitude. Imagine that you aren't looking to get a job but simply seeking a place to share your talents and gifts. Look for ways you can give something of value (your core competencies) to an organization, person, place, or thing.

b. From this frame of mind, experiment with the following ways to research. Try asking the universe to show you where you're skills are needed at this time. Be specific in your intention. Research away from your computer at least 50% of the time!

   o Go to job search sites such as www.monster.com, www.craigslist.com, and www.careerbuilder.com. Explore career planning resources or available positions. Consider any job that interests you regardless of salary, history, or experience.
   o Look in your Yellow Pages for companies that seem interesting or those that you'd like to learn more about.
   o Check out Web sites of companies you admire.
   o Talk to friends, colleagues, and family members for ideas.
   o Go to the library and read magazines aligned with your field.
   o Learn about the difference between for-profit and not-for-profit.
   o Call five recruiters or headhunters to get the scoop on their services and how they work.
   o Drive around town and see what buildings or companies attract you.
   o Directly confront the "I'll just work for myself" idea by taking Brent Bowers' self-assessment in his book "8 Patterns of Highly Effective Entrepreneurs"
   o Go to your favorite bookstore and peruse career planning books such as "What Color Is Your Parachute" by Richard Nelson Bolles.
   o Travel.

- Talk to small-business owners to better understand the risk and challenges of owning your own business.
- Hang out in a coffee shop and read the want ads.
- Take a training, self-development, or college class.
- Volunteer in a field or organization you're interested in.
- Take a temp job to try out different companies.
- Ask for information regarding your career in your dreams each night. Use Gayle Delaney's methods to access your own wisdom from "Living Your Dreams."
- Notice coincidences and synchronicities and follow the clues.
- Identify all the requirements for the work you seek.
- Get ideas from career planning Web sites such as these:
  - www.mindtools.com/pages/article/newISS_01.htm
  - www.khake.com/page51.html
  - www.careerplanner.com/
  - www.bls.gov/k12/index.htm
- Google key words and surf the net.
- Visit a career resources center at a high school, a university, or your alma mater.
- Ask for information in your dreams each night before you go to bed. When you wake up write down your dream and see if it has any helpful clues.
- Throw one of Barbara Sher's Idea Parties (www.barbarasher.com).
- Identify five people you admire and interview them to see how they made it.
- Watch documentaries to recognize the challenge inherent in success.
- Do something out of your comfort zone each day.
- Drive a different way to the grocery store each week.
- Vary your work schedule. Eat lunch with someone new.
- Check out free career services through the YMCA. www.ymca.com
- Talk to people on the bus, on the plane, or in the grocery store. Ask questions such as, "What's the most fun about being in your occupation?" "What's the craziest thing that's ever happened at work?" "Who are some people you admire and why?" "What trends are you seeing?"
- Check out trends and which ones you can fill a need in (www.faithpopcorn.com).
- Walk around Target® or Safeway™ and see what ideas pop into your head.
- Schedule informational interviews.
- Send a letter to people in your network listing the top 10 companies you want to work for and asking whether they'd be willing to share an inside contact.
- Ask three people how they landed their current job.
- Research companies in your industry that have challenges and come up with ways to resolve them.
- Explore the site www.fireproofyourcareer.com.

At this time, I'm attracted to the following positions or opportunities …

Resources
Books and Web Sites
Looking for a job?

- o "In Search of the Perfect Job: 8 Steps to the $250,000+ Executive Job That's Right for You" by Clyde Lowstuter
- o "Knock 'Em Dead 2008" by Martin Yate
- o www.6figurejobs.com
- o www.backdoorjobs.com
- o www.careerbuilder.com
- o www.careerplanner.com
- o http://www.careerperfect.com/content/career-planning-work-preference-inventory
- o www.craigslist.org
- o www.dice.com
- o www.improvenow.com
- o www.indeed.com
- o www.jobbankusa.com
- o www.jobdiagnosis.com
- o www.job-hunt.org
- o www.jobing.com
- o www.livecareer.com
- o www.monster.com
- o www.preferredjobs.com
- o www.quintcareers.com
- o www.theladders.com
- o www.usajobs.gov

Looking for a job and you're over 50?

- o "Encore: Finding Work That Matters in the Second Half of Life" by Marc Freedman
- o www.aarp.org
- o www.aarp.org/money/careers/findingajob/featuredemployers/info.html
- o www.encore.com
- o www.fiveoclockclub.com
- o www.retirementjobs.com
- o www.worforce50.com

Looking to start your own business?

- o See resources and ideas on pages 60-63.

Looking for nonprofit work?

- o www.civicventures.com
- o www.opportunityknocks.org
- o www.philanthropy.com
- o www.nonprofitjobs.org
- o www.nonprofitoyster.com
- o www.nptjobs.com

Looking for education, volunteer, or travel opportunities?

- o www.ambassadorsforchildren.org
- o www.betterworldclub.com
- o www.crossculturalsolutions.org
- o www.earthwatch.org
- o www.experiencecorps.org
- o www.habitatt.org/gv
- o www.kiva.org
- o www.lonelyplanet.com
- o www.responsibletravel.com
- o www.semesteratsea.com
- o www.upwithpeople.org
- o www.vocationvacation.com
- o www.VillageBanking.org
- o www.writersdigest.org

Looking for green jobs?

- o www.catamountinstitute.org
- o www.ecoemploy.com
- o www.ecojobs.com
- o www.environmentalcareers.com
- o www.envorinmentaljobs.com
- o www.greenbiz.com
- o www.greencareercentral.com
- o www.greenenergy/jobs.com
- o www.greenfootjobs.com
- o www.sustainablebuisness.com/jobs
- o www.sustainableindustries.com/jobs

Action

I commit to doing/being/thinking _____ as a result of my discoveries.

"If a window of opportunity appears, don't pull down the shade."
— Tom Peters

Tap Your Network

The people you interact with frequently and infrequently in all aspects of your life make up your network. This includes your acquaintances, companions, colleagues, friends, and relations. More specifically, your network consists of people in associations; community, business, or spiritual organizations; sporting groups; e-mail address book contacts; online social groups; book clubs; family members; and classmates.

If you include your network in your career exploration, you'll not only learn about your impact but you'll also increase your visibility and exposure. These people can help you uncover and articulate ways you add value, and they may even open a door or two. Word of mouth is the most effective advertising.

Inquiry

1. Whom do you know and what organizations are they involved with? (List everyone.)

2. What services or competencies can you offer each person on your list?

3. What online social networks can you participate in (LinkedIn, FaceBook, MySpace, Plaxo Pulse, Skillwho.com)?

4. Whom can you ask for help? How will you do this?

Exercise Network Map

a. Sit upright in your chair with some space in front of you. Separate your knees, fold your upper body over your legs, and let your head and arms fall gently toward the floor. Close your eyes and let your mind go blank while you take five deep breaths. Pause and sit up slowly.

b. Illuminate your connections. Use the sample below as a guide to create your own network map on the next page.

    i.   Draw a circle and put your name in the center.

    ii.   Add circles around your circle to represent all the organizations or groups of people in your life.

    iii.   Place the group circles in relation to you by closeness and importance, and then draw a line linking them to you.

    iv.   Label each of the circles with the organization, school, group, team, or association you're affiliated with or have been involved with in the past.

    v.   For each group circle, add new lines and a new circle with a person's name that is related to that group or team. Add as many as you can think of for each group circle.

    vi.   When you're done, look at your network map and identify who might be available for job leads, informational interviews, or brainstorming.

Network Map Sample

Your Network Map

I've identified the following people in my network whom I can call or e-mail with a request, idea, or offering …

Resources
Books
- o "Guerrilla Marketing" by Jay Conrad Levinson
- o "I'm on LinkedIn — Now What?" by Jason Alba
- o "Plug Your Business: Marketing on MySpace, YouTube, Blogs, Podcasts and Other Social Networking Sites" by Steve Weber
- o "Social Networking" by Jay Leibowitz
- o "Word of Mouth Marketing" by Andy Sernovitz

Web Sites
- o www.careerjournal.com/jobhunting/networking/
- o www.facebook.com
- o www.friendster.com
- o www.jibbberjobber.com
- o www.linkndin.com
- o www.netimpact.org
- o www.managementhelp.org/mrktng/mrktng.htm
- o www.marketingpower.com/
- o www.myspace.com
- o www.rileyguide.com/network.html
- o www.zaadz.com

Other References
- o High school and college reunions and committees
- o Associations: www.seekingsuccess.com/assoc.php3alumni or www.ipl.org/div/aon/

Action

I commit to doing/being/thinking _____ as a result of my discoveries.

"I've found that luck is quite predictable. If you want more luck, take more chances. Be more active. Show up more often." — Brian Tracy

Create a Value Proposition

It's critical to understand your market and the customers you serve best. Fill a niche in your profession or field of contribution as if you were a business. Articulate what you offer specifically in terms of what an employer, customer, or client needs.

Consider how you add value and what your service is worth monetarily in the context of what's needed and what services you provide. It's easier to negotiate a mutually beneficial salary or fee if you frame your proposition in a way that's "bringing to" versus "taking from."

Inquiry

1. What services, products, skills, or competencies do you provide?

2. Who are your potential customers, clients, or employers? How would you describe them? What do they need and want? Where is their pain? What problems can you help solve?

3. What does the marketplace buy from you or hire you for? What makes you unique?

4. What are your features (characteristics), advantages (what a feature offers), and benefits (why an employee will hire you or customer will buy your services)?

5. What are the results you can deliver worth (hourly, daily, project rate, or compensation package)? For employment deals include the dollar value of benefits, vacation/sick pay, and perks.

Exercise Value Proposition

a. Sit quietly and smile. Lift up the corners of your mouth and open your eyes. Imagine your toes, belly, and heart are smiling, and then go back to your face. Notice what happens to your energy level and emotional state. Bring this smile to crafting your value proposition.

b. A value proposition is a concise statement that focuses on how your offering (competencies/skills) fill a specific need (in a unique, compelling manner) such that you make it easy for someone to buy (to hire you). Get clear on your value exchange to enhance your chance of landing a job or gig. Using the two circles below, consider the relationship between your niche and your potential employer/client needs.

   i. In one circle, list your top five competencies (page 54), values (page 39) and salary range including benefits/perks or fees. Consider your specialized offerings or niche.

   ii. In the other circle, list the needs, aspirations, values, and salary range or budget of your targeted employers or clients. The overlap (where the circles intersect) is where you'll find the best ideas for articulating and adding value.

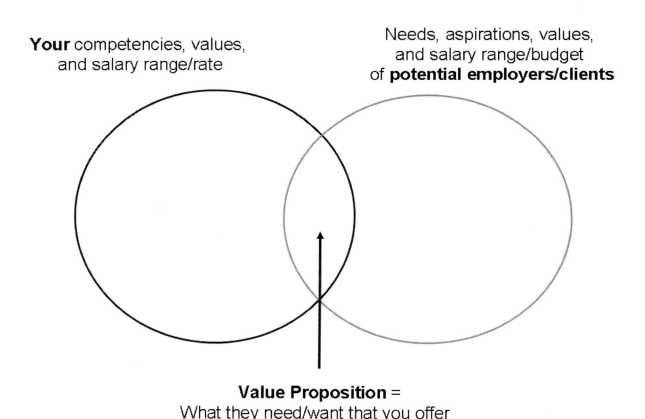

Value Proposition =
What they need/want that <u>you</u> offer

My value proposition is …

Resources

Books

- "Attraction Marketing" by Annie Meachem
- "Law of Attraction" by Michael J. Losier
- "The Energy of Money" by Maria Nemeth
- "The Law of Attraction" by Esther and Jerry Hicks
- "The Soul of Money" by Lynne Twist
- "Value-Based Fees" by Alan Weiss

Web Sites

- www.blendedvalue.org
- http://career.berkeley.edu/Infolab/Salary.stm
- www.collegegrad.com/careers/all.shtml
- www.fastcompany.com
- www.marketingprofs.com
- www.marketvaluesolutions.com
- www.mindtools.com (practical creativity)
- www.payscale.com
- http://www.quintcareers.com/salary_package.html
- www.salaryexpert.com/index.cfm?FuseAction=Home.career-salaries
- www.signalrockcomm.com (Kathy VanBuskirk)

Action

I commit to doing/being/thinking _____ as
a result of my discoveries.

"Price is what you pay. Value is what you get." — Warren Buffett

Refine Your Résumé

A résumé is a marketing tool designed to make it easy for employers to fill positions. Describe yourself as if you were a brand such as Pepsi®, Whole Foods®, or Honda®. Be explicit about what makes you unique and what you offer.

Format your résumé for the industry or type of work you're pursuing. Include a summary of qualifications that communicate your core competencies, your years of experience, and the industries in which you've worked. Be sure you convey specific skills, tangible results you delivered (instead of all the tasks you performed), employment history, and education and training highlights.

You'll hear many opinions on résumé writing. Do your research, and align the content with the type of work you seek. Differentiate, stay integral, and listen to your own voice the most.

Inquiry

1. How does your current résumé make you feel? (Check all that apply.)

    ❏Terrified ❏Worried ❏Embarrassed ❏ Ready ❏ Competent ❏Proud

2. Does the expertise that your résumé highlights match the kind of work you want more of?

3. Who has been attracted to your résumé? Who hasn't?

4. What specific outcomes (including statistics and financial impact) did you deliver that set you apart?

Exercise Writing/Updating Your Résumé

a. Sit up tall in your chair and lift your shoulders up and down toward your ears and away from your ears slowly. Then bow your head (chin to chest) when your shoulders are up and look up releasing your head back gently as your shoulders are down. Move deliberately for a few minutes and breathe deeply as you do so.

b. Go to a career site such as www.careerstrides.com and look at résumés in your niche. If you're an executive or an aspiring executive, go to www.executiveresume.com. Use what the site suggests regarding your career arena. Find a template that meets the needs of the industry or organization in which you're looking for work, as well as your own instinct. If you're pursuing educational, corporate, or government work, research the job requirements and use the résumé format and hiring protocols exactly. Two common formats are functional and chronological.

A functional or skills-based résumé is structured by competencies to highlight your skills and experience. You still provide your work history in bullet format.

NAME AND CONTACT INFORMATION

SUMMARY

- Number of years experience in what field or type of work with what types of organizations or in what industries
- Five words that capture your values, uniqueness, or approach

SKILLS AND EXPERIENCE

- List top five to seven competencies.
- For each competency, list one to three results, outcomes, or examples of something you accomplished using this skill.
- Start each point with a verb (developed, started, created, designed, operated, produced, managed, organized, promoted, etc.).
- Ensure that content supports/validates your summary.

EMPLOYMENT HISTORY

- List job title, organization name, location, and employment date ranges.

EDUCATION AND TRAINING

- List credentials, educational degrees, and training or certification programs. Include dates and locations.

COMMUNITY SERVICE (optional)

- List volunteer experience with job title, organization, location, and dates.

A <u>chronological or historical résumé</u> illuminates your skills and results in the context of your work history.

NAME AND CONTACT INFORMATION

SUMMARY

- Number of years experience in what field or type of work with what types of organizations or in what industries
- Five words that capture your values, uniqueness, or approach

WORK EXPERIENCE

- List job title, company worked for, location, and employment date ranges.
- Under each position, list results, outcomes, or examples of something you accomplished using this skill. Start each point with a verb (developed, started, created, designed, operated, produced, managed, etc.).
- Ensure that content supports/validates your summary.

EDUCATION AND TRAINING

- List credentials, educational degrees, and training or certification programs. Include dates and locations.

COMMUNITY SERVICE (optional)

- List volunteer experience with job title, organization, location, and dates.

---

c. Turn your attention to your own résumé. Complete each section of the résumé template you selected that best meets the needs of they type of employment you seek.

d. When you have a draft, use the following résumé checklist to ensure your résumé has clarity, personality, value, and aliveness. If this process becomes overwhelming or you need more help, hire a résumé writing professional or get input from a headhunter in your field.

Résumé Checklist

Clarity: Make it easy to read.

- ❑ Format in one page with summary and bullet points (except for academic or executive).
- ❑ Use good grammar and ensure there are no typos.
- ❑ Share the facts in words and numbers that are accurate, clear, meaningful, and targeted.
- ❑ Eliminate redundancy and duplication.
- ❑ Highlight skills, capabilities, qualifications, results, and unique contributions.

Personality: Share yourself.

- ❑ Come up with five words that reflect the way in which you work.
- ❑ Evoke your talents, gifts, passions, values, and desired impact.
- ❑ Avoid listing everything you can do. Instead, zero in on the type of work you want more of.
- ❑ Be sure your résumé resonates and aligns with your essence (who you really are).

Value: Fill a need.

- ❑ Articulate the ways you fulfill specific and general industry needs.
- ❑ Use a format (functional, chronological, or curriculum vitae) and language required for the position/organization/work you seek.
- ❑ Convert experiences into tangible skills that reflect your value proposition.
- ❑ Create insightful, value-added talking points that you can use in interviews to support line items in your résumé.

Aliveness: Light up your message.

- ❑ Select dynamic (not flowery) and reflective words that capture your value.
- ❑ Provide rich examples and specific differentiators.
- ❑ Ask for and integrate feedback from friends, cohorts, and interviewers.
- ❑ Express yourself authentically (don't lie or fudge the truth).

My résumé will attract ...

Resources

Books

- ° "Knock 'em Dead Resumes" by Martin Yates
- ° "Resume Magic" by Susan Britton Whitcomb
- ° "The Resume Handbook" by Arthur Rosenberg

Web Sites

- o www.amazon.com (Search "résumé.")
- o www.aarp.org/money/careers/findingajob/resumes/a2004-05-28-rightresume.html
- o www.careerknowhow.com
- o www.cvtips.com/resume.html
- o www.executiveresume.com
- o www.google.com (Search "résumé" and add terms such as "functional," "chronological," and "curriculum vitae.")
- o www.grammargirl.com
- o http://hotjobs.yahoo.com/resume
- o www.jobbankusa.com
- o http://jobsearch.about.com/od/resumes/Resumes.htm
- o http://jobstar.org/tools/resume/index.php
- o www.myresumeonline.org
- o www.recruitersdirectory.com/
- o www.recruitersonline.com/
- o www.resumebroadcaster.com/
- o www.resumes.com
- o www.resumegator.com/pages/job-sites.asp

Action

I commit to doing/being/thinking _____ as
a result of my discoveries.

"If I keep my mind focused on peace, harmony, health, love, and
abundance, then I can't be distracted by doubt, anxiety, and fear."
— Edith Armstrong

Develop Talking Points

In career transition whether you're negotiating for a job, playing on a tennis court, or shopping in the grocery store, you're interviewing all the time. What do you want people to remember about you? Prepare for formal and informal interactions so you can be spontaneous and authentic instead of scripted.

Talking points are true career stories, examples, and highlights you choose to share with people about your transition or job search. Plan what you want to communicate before people ask (especially if you're uncomfortable, nervous, or worried). In formal interviews, be ready to answer behavioral interviewing questions such as, "Tell me about a time when ..." and, "If I asked your manager about your performance, how would she respond?" Do your homework and know your limits so you can handle salary and benefit questions with ease.

Strive to differentiate yourself from the pack. Focus attention on all the ways you add value. Remember to bring your own list of questions as you are interviewing potential employers and clients as much as they are interviewing you!

Inquiry

1. What's compelling about your profession?

2. What are some common interview questions you can anticipate?

3. What are all the career transition and job search questions you're afraid people will ask you professionally and socially? Write them down; then spend some time to answer each one for yourself!

4. What's your elevator speech, your compelling one-sentence reply to the question, "So what do you do?"

Exercise Talking Points

a. Do a few of the word puzzles below to get your creative brain engaged. Verbalize the phonics and guess the person, place, or thing. You'll find the answers after the Resources section.

 1. Docked Hearse Whose (children's book author)   _____
 2. The Hound Dove Moo Sick (classic movie)   _____
 3. Sand Tack Laws (beloved character)   _____
 4. Age Ant Hub Blows Heaven (movie character)   _____

b. Look at your résumé and the results you identified for each position (chronological) or skill (functional). For each tangible result you accomplished or contributed, write a specific example or story conveying the impact of your work on the quality, service, or cost of your team and your department, as well as your organization and its customers. For example:

 ° If your result is, "Implemented 100 projects with budgets of $250,000 to $500,000 with a 95% budget/time adherence," write a brief story about a time you almost missed a deadline and what you did to keep on track.

 ° If your result is, "Discovered over 25 new uses for trash/recycled/marginal materials and air pollution control technologies using waste oil, tire recycling, and small diameter wood," share one experience you had in the discovery process that was challenging, or share what excited you about the work itself. Add some interesting details.

c. Fill in the table below with some of your own talking points. Express not just what you did, but the way in which you achieved a specific result and the impact that you had. A good story is not a bland fact you give by rote; it's a relevant, descriptive, and attention-grabbing chronicle. It's not arrogant or embellished, but honest with some suspense. An interesting example draws in a listener and compels him/her to want to know more.

 Once you make your list, practice at parties, in front of the mirror, and during interviews. Have someone video you for helpful information about how you present!

Result	Compelling Example/Story

The most compelling thing I can talk about regarding my career is …

Resources
Books
- o "101 Great Answers to the Toughest Interview Questions" by Ron Fry
- o "Give Your Elevator Speech a Lift" by Lorraine Howell

Web Sites
- o www.americanventuremagazine.com/articles/369/
- o www.creativekeys.net/PowerfulPresentations/article1024.html
- o http://www.jobinterviewquestions.org/
- o http://jobsearch.about.com/od/interviewquestionsanswers/a/interviewquest.htm
- o www.mandelcomm.com
- o www.quintcareers.com/writing_elevator_speeches.html
- o http://www.quintcareers.com/career_doctor_cures/job_interview_questions.html
- o www.storyarts.com
- o www.writersdigest.com

Other
Lisa Mouscher, behavioral interviewing coach, (303) 709-1534

Answers to word play: Dr. Seuss, The Sound of Music, Santa Claus, Agent 007.

Action

I commit to doing/being/thinking _____ as
a result of my discoveries.

"If you want to get clients (or employers), you have to talk to them."
— CJ Hayden

Target Cover Letters

Cover letters are a targeted version of your talking points for a specific position or job opening. Use cover letters to explicitly illuminate specific skills, interests, and contributions. Connect the dots for the reader by briefly explaining how one or two of your skills meet the criteria of the position opening.

Think of cover letters like the headline of a great article. Instead of recapping your résumé or sharing empty accolades, illuminate what you know about the organization and how you might best contribute. Create interest. State your value proposition clearly, and then invite the reader to consider your request graciously with a call to action.

Inquiry

1. What excites you about the position or type of work you're seeking?

2. What urgent challenges is your industry, nation, or company going through at this time?

3. What professional tone or writing style reflects the real you?

Exercise Writing a Cover Letter

a. Consider the company you're hoping to work for or with. Imagine what it would be like to work for the company. See yourself going to the work setting. How are you contributing? What difference is your presence making? How are customers responding to you or your work? If you can't see yourself there, go to the company's Web site, or call someone who works inside or knows about the organization. Look for and discuss challenges, goals, values, trends, and needs.

b. Research different cover letter styles. Get ideas from the resources section in this workbook, or use the outline below to create a cover letter template to use as the basis for all your communications.

   i. Open: Introduce yourself and how you found out about the opportunity.

   ii. Body: One or two specific skills you have that match the position description and/or ways you might contribute to the organization's challenges.

iii.   Close: A call to action and a thank you for consideration.

c. Once you have a draft, invite a friend or colleague to copy-edit it and check for clarity, readability, tone, grammar, and punctuation. Do so with each letter you send.

If I received my own cover letter I'd feel and think…

Resources
Books
- "Cover Letters for Dummies" by Joyce Kennedy
- "Dynamic Cover Letters" by Katherine and Randall Hansen
- "Overnight Job Change Letter" by Donald Asher
- "The Complete Idiot's Guide to the Perfect Cover Letter" by Susan Ireland
- "Win Without Competing: Career Success the Right Fit Way" Dr. Arlene Barro

Web Sites
- www.bestcoverletters.com
- http://www.collegegrad.com/coverletters/
- www.grammargirl.com
- http://jobstar.org/tools/resume/cletters.php
- http://jobsearch.about.com/od/coverletters/Cover_Letters.htm

Action

I commit to doing/being/thinking _____ as a result of my discoveries.

"Success is a ladder you cannot climb with your hands in your pockets."
— American proverb

Update Your Looks

First impressions matter. In fact, most interpersonal communication is 80% nonverbal. Presence, the energy of you, needs to reflect how you dress, stand, move, and speak. You can't fake this! Interviewers are checking to see that your essence and form match a given position.

People do make assumptions about how you might perform a job based on your appearance and how they feel in your presence. If you're neat and tidy, you might produce reports without typos. If you slouch, you might be careless with equipment. If your clothes are current, you may be up to date on market trends. If, behind a smile, you're filled with anxiety, you may scare away customers. The more comfortable you are with your whole being — body, mind, and sprit — the more others will be too.

Inquiry

1. How would a video camera record your professional "look"?

2. What is the professional style of your chosen occupation or career field?

3. If you met yourself for the first time, what assumptions would you make about yourself in the first five minutes based on how you look, sound, act, and feel?

4. How does your external appearance illuminate your true self?

Exercise The Look of You

a. Put on some music you love and dance as if no one is watching. If you can't think of a song, try "Dance to the Music" by Sly and The Family Stone. For three minutes, let yourself move freely without worrying what you look like or without judging your performance.

b. Look at yourself in a full-length mirror or have someone videotape you talking and walking. Honestly assess your physical being and presence. Answer the following questions. If you get stuck, hire an image consultant to help you claim your assets and update your appearance.

i. What do you notice about yourself first? Second? Third?
ii. What do you love about your appearance? What bothers you?
iii. How does your body type serve you and the work you seek?
iv. What is your personal style?
v. What's current about your wardrobe, hairstyle, posture, and face? What isn't?
vi. What clothes illuminate or interfere with your authentic self? Are you hiding, showing off, or simply real?
vii. What does the quality of your voice reveal?

I'll change/accept the following about my professional appearance...

Resources

Books

- "Blink" by Malcom Gladwell
- "40 Over 40" by Brenda Kinsel
- "First Impressions: What You Don't Know About How Others See You" By Ann Demarias
- "Heading South?" by Sue Donnelly
- "How Not to Look Old" by Charla Krupp
- "Staging Your Comeback" by Christopher Hopkins

Web Sites

- www.aici.org/
- www.dressforsuccess.com
- http://hbswk.hbs.edu/item/4860.html
- www.newyorkimageconsultant.com/
- www.racheldee.com
- www.tlc.discovery.com/fansites/whatnottowear/stylegurus/london.html

Action

I commit to doing/being/thinking _____ as a result of my discoveries.

"How things look on the outside of us depends on how things are on the inside of us." – Park Cousins

V. Live Your Future, Today

This section focuses on habits and practices for productive and engaging career transition. The concepts enable you to stay present to the moments of each day, to the opportunities that come your way, and to your own innate wisdom. The more consciously you respond (instead of reacting) to what's right in front of you, the more successful you'll be at staying on the career path meant for you!

- Intend to Serve
- Plan for Magic
- Make Conscious, Aligned Choices
- Anticipate Resistance
- Celebrate Daily

"Put your whole self in … that is commitment. Put your whole self out … that is detachment. Then turn yourself around … that is transformation and that's what it's all about." — Swami Beyondananda

Intend to Serve

Focus on what you want by clarifying your intentions. Intentions are like goals, but they leave space for the unexpected and include something bigger than you. State specifically what you want to create as if you already have it. Intentions invite you to articulate what you'd like to see, have, and experience in your career in the context of service.

A meaningful intention is conscious, SMART, and in service. "Conscious" means that you're aware of what you're going for, you've considered the impact and constraints, and you've included your higher self. "SMART" means that your objectives are described in such a way that is **s**pecific, **m**easurable, **a**chievable, **r**elevant, and **t**ime-bounded. "In service" means that your wish benefits humanity in some manner.

This clarity ensures that when you get what you want, it'll be fulfilling, lasting, and in service to more than just your ego.

Inquiry

1. What do you really want to create?

2. Who benefits (including yourself) and how?

3. What's your current assignment, sacred contract, or focus?

4. What's enough? Money, title, hours a week, contribution, etc.?

Exercise Creating SMART Intentions/Goals

a. Ask yourself, "What do I want to be or do in terms of serving, helping, or creating?" Then do a series of physical movements while your mind receives answers. Stand on a chair for a minute, and then lie on the floor for two minutes. Now stand up and turn around slowly, spinning like a top. Sit in a rocking chair and rock. Finally, do five jumping jacks. Notice what ideas come to mind.

b. Write down what you want in the gray box below. Think about what you can give instead what you can get. Consider what you want to create or deliver that will benefit someone or something else. Make your intention very clear and alive by converting your intention to a SMART (specific, measurable, achievable, relevant, time-bounded) goal. Articulate the who, what, why, where, and when of your intention as if you already had it. Use the table below as a guide.

I want to make lots of money.	I have $200,000 in my bank account from 50 invoices from enlightened purchasing agents for air purification products that improve air quality in U.S. corporate offices by Oct. 1.
I want to help people.	I secured housing and provided financial education for 50 hard-working, low-income families who are willing to learn by Jan. 15.
I want to help the environment.	My small-business recycling program is operating in 100 retail stores, making it easy to recycle packaging materials and saving three hours of work time a week.
I want to write.	Baby boomers are learning how to fall in love with life again by reading my book. Sales are generating $50,000, which is helping pay for my children's college tuition.
I want to make a difference.	I serve 50 customers a day on the phone providing technical support in a kind, generous, and "teach 'em how to fish" manner.
I want to …	

My career intention/goal is….

Resources

Books

- o "As a Man Thinketh" by James Allen
- o "Coaching for Performance" by John Whitmore (GROW model)
- o "Rich Dad, Poor Dad" by Robert Kiyosaki
- o "Performance Coaching" by John Whitmore
- o "Sacred Contracts" by Carolyn Myss
- o "Theory U" by C. Otto Scharmer

Web Sites

- o www.abraham-hicks.com
- o www.anticareer.com
- o www.briantracy.com
- o http://careerplanning.about.com/
- o www.carolynmyss.com
- o www.dreamsalive.com
- o www.goal-setting-guide.com
- o www.greenleaf.org/
- o www.goal-setting-guide.com
- o www.sheldrake.org
- o www.suzeorman.com
- o www.ziglar.com

Action

I commit to doing/being/thinking _____ as a result of my discoveries.

"Progress is impossible without change, and those who cannot change their minds cannot change anything." — George Bernard Shaw

Plan for Magic

Your career intention acts like a magnet; it will attract opportunities to you. Plan for and take action that aligns with your goal. Try not to force, manipulate, or play games with yourself as you step up and step out. Remain in a calm state of readiness like an athlete poised for the next play. Move when you're inspired and pause to reflect when you are not. Notice how everything in creation is supporting you and illuminating your path.

Planning for the magic means that you act and allow, confront and surrender, schedule and leave space, give and receive, get and let go. You notice and respond to what the universe is showing you while you move in the direction of your dreams. You take action from a place of awareness instead of fear. Doors will open and close. Trust the process.

Inquiry

1. What one action is right in front of you that you can take today to move toward your career goal?

2. What one step that you don't want to take that will move you closer to your career aspiration?

3. What constraints or barriers do you need to acknowledge and plan for?

4. What training or development to you need to achieve your career goal?

Exercise Action Planning (To Dos and Practices)

a. Stand up and feel your feet firmly on the ground. If you can, take off your shoes and socks. Stand tall and hold up your shoulders. Notice how your feet are contacting the floor. Imagine you're plugging them into the floor. Lift up your big toes in the air, off the floor, while keeping your other toes on the ground. Then rest. Now keep your big toes on the floor while you lift the other toes. Go back and forth for a minute or so. Notice how your feet are contacting the floor now.

b. To ground your actions in reality, start by restating your career intention/goal in the table below. Then, in the Deliverables column, break down your career intention/goal into smaller parts. Write down the tangible and specific components of your main goal.

c. In the Action column, identify the specific tasks that will produce the deliverable you identified. Create your to-do list by looking at each deliverable that makes up your career goal and listing all the steps you can take to achieve it. Don't forget to build in strategies to deal with constraints and barriers. Get creative.

d. When you've identified a list of actions for each aspect of your goal, consider the impact of your list. What will be different? How will you know? Why does it matter? Note these in the What Will Be Different column. This is a good way to check that your action plan is relevant, aligned, and motivating to you.

e. Finally consider daily practices or habits that will keep you in a state of readiness to know when to act and when to remain still. What can you do to embody your vision, mission, values, and competencies as you tackle your to dos? How will you stay in a "service" frame of mind? What activities help you stay neutral and calm? What mindsets do you need to reinforce? How will you notice universal signs? Note these in the Daily Practices section.

Career Intention/Goal:

Deliverable	Action	What Will Be Different?

Daily Practices:

One action or practice I'll implement today is …

Resources

Books

- o "Live Your Dreams" by Gayle Delaney
- o "Messages From Water" by Masuru Emoto
- o "Speed of Light" by Gwyneth Cravens
- o "Start Late, Finish Rich" by David Bach
- o "Turning To One Another" by Margaret Wheatley

Web Sites

- o www.abraham-hicks.com
- o www.artofconsciouscreation.com
- o www.dreamcoach.com
- o http://healing.about.com/od/marciawieder/a/powerintention.htm
- o www.stevepavlina.com/blog/2006/06/how-intentions-manifest/

Action

I commit to doing/being/thinking _____ as
a result of my discoveries.

"Start close in. Don't take the second step or the third. Start with the first
thing close in, the step you don't want to take." — David Whyte

Make Conscious, Aligned Choices

Create a decision-making checklist to sort through each alternative that comes your way or to examine what attracts you. Take a stand for what matters to you by determining upfront how you'll decide. Consider what's negotiable and what isn't negotiable. Write down what you gain and lose by a given choice to illuminate the whole picture, not just the part you want to see!

The more aware you are when you make a choice, the more the outcome will nourish instead of deplete.

Inquiry

1. What criteria will you use to make good career decisions? (Make a list.)

2. What are the pros and cons of the career choice you are currently facing?

3. Who or what is impacted by your career decisions?

4. What won't you do? What are "deal breakers"?

5. In your career choices, whom do you need to consult with (talk to before a decision) or inform (share a decision with after you made it)?

Exercise Alignment Check

a. Lie down on a carpet and stretch your hands over your head on the floor. Slowly bring your right elbow to your left knee by bending at your elbow and knee. Then in a cross-crawl motion, bring your left elbow to your right knee. Repeat five times and let your head roll gently side to side. Pause a minute then get up slowly.

b. The table below helps you check that your own vision, mission, values, competencies and goals align with an organization you are considering (even if it's your own business). Fill in the first column of the table with your discoveries from previous sections of this workbook. Then add what you know about the organization you are hoping to work with. How compatible are you?

	Me	The Organization
Vision Desired future state (page 34) *What's possible?*	I dream...	We see a world that...
Mission Purpose, calling (page 36) *Why do I/we exist?*	My assignment is...	Our purpose is...
Values Guiding principles (page 39) *What matters?*	I'm motivated by...	We value...
Core Competencies Tangible, marketable skills/services (page 54) *What adds value?*	I bring these skills...	We provide these products/services...
Intentions Goals (page 92) *What are my/our desired results?*	I choose...	We're focused on...

I'm taking a stand for...

Resources
Books
- "Consensus Through Conversation: How to Achieve High-Commitment Decisions" by Larry Dressler
- "Energy Medicine" by Donna Eden
- "Touch for Health" by John Thie
- "Values Based Decision Making" by David Seedhouse

Web Sites
- www.businessballs.com
- www.debbieford.com
- www.kahunakindergarden.com (using a pendulum and muscle testing in the Sharing the Good Stuff section)
- http://www.kinesiology.net/
- www.marthabeck.com
- www.mindtools.com (decision-making techniques)
- www.self.com
- www.successfactors.com
- www.valuescentre.com (values based decision making)

Other References
Explore alternative decision-making methods such as chakra work, numerology, astrology, muscle testing, tarot, and using a pendulum.

Action

I commit to doing/being/thinking _____
as a result of my discoveries.

"What we call the secret of happiness is no more a secret than our willingness to choose life." — Leo Buscaglia

Anticipate Resistance

As you commit to a career goal and start taking steps toward your vision, you may encounter resistance. This is different from the challenges and constraints you identified and built into your career goals. Resistance is any internal thought, feeling, sensation, or conflict that interferes in your ability to fulfill your goals. This energy may or may not have a logical reason, and it may or may not originate within you.

Whether resistance shows up as belief (it's not really possible to make money doing what I love), as fear (I'm not good enough), as conflicting values (financial security and fulfillment), or as someone else's opinion (you can't do that!), ignoring it, whining about it, or fighting it can be counterproductive. The depth of your desire often equals the size of your resistance, so expect it and learn from it.

Inquiry

1. What internal voices are getting louder as you pursue your career goals?

2. What fears do you have about your career intentions and strategies?

3. What is the origin of these fears and what might they be trying to communicate?

4. How will you choose growth and risk instead of comfort and relief?

Exercise Confronting "Yeah, Buts"

a. Go to www.thedailyshow.com for Jon Stewart or
   http://www.comedycentral.com/shows/the_colbert_report/index.jhtml for Stephen
   Colbert. Watch and listen to a video. Laugh out loud.

b. Consider wherever you are in your career journey and listen to your internal dialogue. What "yeah, buts" do you hear? When you look at your career goal, action plan, and decision-making list, what comes up in your consciousness? Look for statements that start with, "I could, **but** … , " "I want to serve, **but** … ," "I have the talent, **but** … ," "I'm ready, **but** … ." Make a list of all your "yeah, buts" below.

c. Imagine that each "yeah, but" you listed above is coming to you with a message. It could be your inner two-year old with a helpful hint. It might be a parental opinion or a religious doctrine with an idea that is outdated or inaccurate. Read each "yeah but" aloud and pretend you are interviewing it as if it were a person. Be curious and open to the information. Some "yeah, buts" have useful information and some are simply crying wolf. Some of the voices originate with you and some are old recordings from your parents, friends, history, family, society, etc. It's your job to listen, discern, and choose what "yeah, but" you give power to. The loudest and most persistent voices are not necessarily the wisest, but they do deserve your ear. Bring all the "yeah, but" wisdom to the surface to determine which voices are helping you and which are interfering in your progress!

I'm doing the following to address my "yeah, buts …"

Resources
Books
- o "Embracing Our Selves" by Hal and Sidra Stone
- o "Loving What Is" by Katie Byron
- o "Taming Your Gremlin" by Rick Carson
- o "The WAR of ART: Winning the Inner Creative Battle" by Steven Pressfield

Web Sites
- o www.appreciative-inquiry.org
- o www.creativethink.com
- o www.creativityworkshop.com/
- o www.dealingwithfear.org
- o www.debonogroup.com/6hats.htm
- o www.nisargadatta.net/
- o www.worrydoll.com

Action

I commit to doing/being/thinking _____ as
a result of my discoveries.

"You often create by default, for you are getting what you are giving your attention to, wanted or unwanted." — Esther Hicks

Celebrate Daily

Decide how you want to track your success, acknowledge your work efforts, and celebrate. Instead of waiting until you've reached your career goal or expecting someone else to recognize your hard work, applaud the actions you implement and the milestones you achieve each day. Look for all the gifts you receive, especially the unexpected ones. Catch yourself doing something right.

This practice creates a state of awe, wonder, and possibility — even during difficult times. Gratefulness can remind you that you're lucky to be here on earth. It keeps your attention on what's working instead of what isn't.

Inquiry

1. Who helped you move closer to your career goals recently?

2. How did a person, place, or thing (including the universe) show you something you needed to learn or give you direction/support that enabled you to keep focused on your career dreams?

3. How did your support system encourage you today?

4. How did your physical, emotional, mental, or spiritual body serve you today?

Exercise Daily Thanks

a. Perform a random act of kindness. Put a quarter in a meter in a parking lot. Call a friend to tell her how much she means to you. Bag your own groceries. Thank a customer service rep for working on a Sunday. Put a chocolate bar in the mailbox for your postal carrier. Weed your garden. Do a chore for your spouse. Compliment a neighbor's improvement project. Send an e-mail to a politician who is supporting your favorite cause. Pet your dog. Send $20 to a niece or nephew. Call a local charity and thank them for the work they do. Give a hug to a friend.

b. Using a journal, notebook, or day planner, write the date on a blank page. Review your day and consider everything that took place.

c. Think about the events, the people, your feelings, the environment, and your actions. Make a list of anything and everything (big and small) that you're thankful for. Here are some tips to consider as you write down what you are thankful for each day:

- List things you did that moved you toward your career goals, where you expressed your values or lived your mission.
- Start simple, such as, "a smile from a child," "the sun on a tree," "a lead from a colleague," or "a kind receptionist."
- Identify behavior changes such as, "I focused on my strengths in the job interview," or "I called Tony to ask for career advice."
- Consider what matters to you. "I created a work of art," or "I had a meaningful conversation." If nothing comes to mind, look at constants such as, "I got out of bed," "the sun came up," or "my heart is beating."

d. Implement this practice every night for a month. Observe what happens to your mood, your days, your career, and your life. Whatever you write down is fine. Sometimes it flows and sometimes it doesn't.

I'm grateful for …

Resources
Books
- "Peace Is Every Step" by Thich Nhat Hanh
- "Simple Abundance" by Sarah Ban Breathnach

Web Sites
- www.cafegratitude.com
- www.greatday.com
- www.foundationforabetterlife.org
- www.mayangelou.com
- www.storycorps.org

Action
I commit to doing/being/thinking _____ as a result of my discoveries.

"Every day we are engaged in a miracle which we don't even recognize: a blue sky, white clouds, green leaves, the black, curious eyes of a child — our own two eyes." — Thich Nhat Hanh

Acknowledgements

The content for "Essentially You @ Work: A Career Transition Guide" is inspired by 20 years of discovery and application of practical business methods, career planning models, and adult learning theory, as well as leading-edge creativity practices, attraction marketing concepts, and human potential teachings in the United States.

Thanks to you (and the work of all my career transition clients) for your willingness to become more aware, conscious, and able to bring your creative best to work!

Thanks to my colleagues and teachers Laura Allard, Norman Allard, Amy Felix-Reese, Stephen Gibbens, Megan Klem, Candace Lienhart, Mariah Martin, Team Coaching International, The Coaches Training Institute and many of the resources listed in this workbook for your commitment to understanding, serving, and facilitating awareness.

Thanks to my content and copy editors Hilary Hatch Copeland and Kathy Snelgrove Phillips for your attention to detail and constant encouragement.

Thanks to my family for your creative expression and enduring love.

Thanks to my former employers and corporate clients, especially Cris Aboussie, Glenna Kelly, and Ronnie Dunleavy O'Conner for your ongoing support and lessons learned.

Want Ongoing Support? For up-to-date career transition resources and inspiration, go to www.brainstormingalamode.com to sign up for our e-letter "The Scoop."

Need Career Transition Coaching? To schedule a 30-minute sample session or sign up for a career coaching series please contact Shawn Snelgrove at (303) 810-1437 or shawn@brainstormingalamode.com.

Looking for Career Transition Coaching for Exiting Employees? To receive volume discounts for this workbook or offer career transition coaching services as part of your organization's severance package, please contact Shawn Snelgrove at (303) 810-1437 or shawn@brainstormingalamode.com.

Brainstorming à la Mode, Inc. provides innovative facilitation, coaching, and consulting services to bring out your creative best.

P.O. Box 1337, Boulder, CO. 80306
(303) 810-1437   www.brainstormingalamode.com

"And, when you realize your true nature…new conditions will flood your experience like quiet rain." –Kristin Zambuka

Resource Index

Go directly to the resource section for each topic to find books, web sites, and other references.